The Whole-Life Confession

Four Weeks of Awakening To Mercy, Healing and Peace

William M. Watson, SJ

# Author's Preface

The Examen and Confession Practice of Ignatius and the First Jesuits

In the early months of his conversion, Ignatius Loyola set off on pilgrimage to the Benedictine monastery of Monserrat. When he arrived, one of the first things he did was make a general confession. He was about thirty years old at the time and the year was 1522. Ignatius spent three days writing out his confession which was customary in that time.

It was his desire to make the confession on the feast of the Annunciation. With the detailed Examination of Conscience (*Examen*) guides written by the Benedictine leader of Monserrat, Abbot Cisneros, every category and shade of sin Ignatius committed in his thirty years could be catalogued, written down, confessed and forgiven.

This begins a life-long practice for Ignatius of both reviewing his life with his own unique form of the *Examen* and his practice of frequent confession. And what St. Ignatius practiced, he made part and parcel of the Society of Jesus' formation process and daily spiritual regimen for all Jesuits.

Like Ignatius' method for training Jesuits, pastoral work with the laity did not shy away from the *Examen's* focus on sin. However the Jesuits sought generally to highlight the more positive aspects of spiritual growth and God's mercy.

The emphasis of Pope Francis' pontificate on mercy is deeply rooted in his Ignatian formation. This positive, mercy-focused approach matched Ignatius' own graced experience of God's love for him as a forgiven sinner. Ignatius said late in his life that he did not think there had been

in the history of the Church someone who had sinned as much as he had who had been given so many graces.

The practice of frequent confession that Ignatius may have learned through Cisneros' writings evolves into a pastoral aid that the early Jesuits widely recommend to all types of people. Its goal was to help an individual "begin to make a new book of one's life." Ignatius' application of the general confession as a review of one's life to aid in spiritual growth caused its acceptance in the wider stream of Catholic practice.

Jesuits offered most of their spiritual direction in the confessional. Many of these early Jesuits would have brought to their confessional ministry the formative experiences of the *Exercises*, where even the meditations on sin in the First Week "were contrived to elicit gratitude."

Learning to Bring *Your Whole* Life to Reconciliation

The Whole-Life Confession is based on Part One of *Forty Weeks: An Ignatian Path to Christ with Sacred Story Prayer*. This very dynamic and holistic method helps you integrate your spiritual, intellectual and psychological/ emotional history. Those who have completed it have been amazed how it helped them "see their whole life" as if for the first time.

The WLC method is grounded in Ignatian spirituality. This means it is focused on helping those who take the journey to access areas of their lives where they need God's healing the most. For some people, this means remembering things they may have pushed out of consciousness. It can create anxiety to encounter experiences from your past. However If they still have energy that upsets you, it means they can greatly benefit from deeper healing by the Divine Physician.

Since the goal of the Whole-Life Confession journey is to bring healing, hope and peace, each person must determine whether they want to take this journey. Some may simply not be ready for it and that is fine.

St. Ignatius' spirituality rests on the interior freedom of the individual. No one can/should be asked to do that which they don't want to do.

But this is the balancing act in making a decision whether to engage the WLC journey. You should make a discernment based on a peaceful heart, not an anxious or fearful heart. The enemy of human nature (St. Ignatius' name for Satan) uses fear to keep us from making choices that bring us closer to God and our own peace. So yes, choose freely, but choose in peacefulness and not from fear. If you proceed with the journey, pay attention to the frequent invitations to say aloud: Be Not Afraid!

To help you make the decision, go to our website: sacredstory.net. Sign up to be a member (it costs nothing) and go to the Member's section. There you will see a heading "FORTY WEEKS – Primary Materials." Click on the document that says: "Experience of the Whole-Life Confession for Participants and Priests." These testimonies will help focus your heart on what you want and desire.

It is my firm conviction that if you learn anew how to make your confession in the method put forth here, and you find a regular confessor for the sacrament (monthly is highly recommended), nearly all the spiritual direction you will need in life will be available to you. Be Not Afraid!

೮೩

℘

"There are very few who realize what God would make
of them if they abandoned themselves entirely to His
hands, and let themselves be formed by His grace. A thick
and shapeless tree trunk would never believe that it could
become a statue, admired as a miracle of sculpture…and
would never consent to submit itself to the chisel of the
sculptor who, as St. Augustine says, sees by his genius
what he can make of it. Many people who, we see, now
scarcely live as Christians, do not understand that they
could become saints, if they would let themselves be
formed by the grace of God, if they did not ruin
His plans by resisting the work which He wants to do."[1]

St. Ignatius Loyola

☙

Introduction

How to Engage *the Whole- Life Confession*

St. Ignatius became a great spiritual guide by surrendering his heart to Christ under the guidance of the Church It is Christ's forgiving and healing love that burns away the selfishness and hardheartedness of sin's legacy in one's history, transforming it into a *Sacred Story*: fruit that endures to eternity.

Following Ignatius's wisdom, all you need to engage this Whole-Life Confession spiritual journey is a generous heart and a willingness to be transformed by Christ's purifying forgiveness and mercy. It is the narrow path to holiness held out by the Church for millennia and the one followed by every saint in our history.

The daily twenty-minute lessons are not complicated. Pray for a generous heart and ask Christ for His help every step of the way. Trusts the wisdom of the structure presented here. Resist the temptation to rush or "pray the weeks" out of their natural order. Simple enough!

෨

Set a Date for the Whole-Life Confession Service

You may be engaging this prayer journey as an individual or as part of a group. If you are doing this by yourself, you may find it beneficial to discipline yourself to schedule the time for your Whole-Life Confession at the beginning of your spiritual journey. We have discovered that it gives great focus to those making a Whole-Life Confession in the same way as those who know the date of a trip they will be making aids their preparation. You say you are not making a trip? Yes you are, and the Whole-Life Confession begins a new book in your spiritual life.

For parishes or faith communities who are doing this together, please go to our website: sacredstory.net and become a Member (it is free). There you will see a heading "FORTY WEEKS – Primary Materials." Click on the document that says: "The Whole-Life Confession Service.". We have discovered a very good method and so take advantage of what we have learned in doing these services.

੪੭

Trust the Process

Trust the process and the rhythm of the spiritual disciplines put forth. They have been tested and proven by thousands of people who have done the Whole-Life Confession process.

If you are part of a group doing these spiritual disciplines, my best advice is to discipline yourself to stay together as a group. That is, keep a 7-day week structure for the whole four weeks. No matter which way you are *undertaking these exercises*—solo or with a group—realize that the exercises are incremental, building on each other.

Doing them slowly and in order will help you stay better focused and live in the present moment. Trust the structure, and do not read or practice the disciplines out of their natural order.

Listen to your heart, at all times, in the present moment. God is *in* the present moment. This way, the Whole-Life Confession journey, by God's grace and your free submission, lead you to the deepest desires of your heart.

੪੭

Lent or Advent

If a faith community using this as a program for Lent, you can begin the Sunday after Ash Wednesday. This will enable you to have your service for the Whole-Life Confession well before Holy Week begins.

If you are doing this for the shorter Advent season, we suggest beginning on the Thirty Third Sunday just before the Feast of Christ the King. This will help you end the liturgical year on a high note and allow you to host the Whole-Life Confession the third week of Advent, a traditional time in many parishes for the Reconciliation before Christmas.

ຂວ

Daily Journal

Acquire for yourself a small notebook or journal for the Whole-Life Confession Journey. If there are no specific journal assignments for a given day, spend two minutes at the end of the exercise and write a short response to each of these two questions: (by "short" we mean ½ to 2 sentences max—no more!).

1) What in the spiritual exercise today increased my faith, hope and love? Be specific and brief.

2) What in the spiritual exercise today decreased my faith, hope and love. Be specific but brief.

ຂວ

Length of Time for Your Daily Spiritual Exercises

For your daily spiritual disciplines—exercises—I suggest you spend no less than fifteen minutes and no more than thirty minutes. Some days have more upon which to reflect and some less. Try to be flexible and be drawn by the Holy Spirit. It may be that on some days you wish to spend longer than thirty minutes. The Holy Spirit will guide you!

ℰ𝒪

"Come to me, all you who labor and are burdened,
and I will give you rest.
Take my yoke upon you and learn from me,
for I am meek and humble of heart;
and you will find rest for your selves.
For my yoke is easy, and my burden light."

Mt 11:28-30

℃ℬ

THREE-DAY PREPARATION FOR
THE WHOLE-LIFE CONFESSION JOURNEY

Take three days to prepare for your Whole-Life Confession journey. For day one, ponder the *Rules of Engagement*. For day two, read one of the four Gospels from beginning to end. And on day three, listen to wisdom on spiritual discernment in the *Sacred Story Affirmations*. And..............
Be Not Afraid!

Preparation Day 1

Rules of Engagement

Welcome to your first preparation day for your spiritual journey. Divine love is an abiding relationship that God invites you to share daily. Listen to the wisdom below to help prepare you to enter this relationship with Christ Jesus in the Whole-Life Confession journey.

✦ If you are looking for quick fixes to spiritual or psychological problems, you will soon lose heart. The full healing of your wounds, and the path to complete peace, only begins on this earth. You will achieve no final victory for what ails you this side of eternity. However you will find the *path* to that final victory and it is here that you will find peace.

✦ If you are being asked to do this spiritual journey to fulfill someone else's plan, or for any sort of program requirement, kindly tell your sponsor, "no thank you." Unless you engage them in complete freedom of heart, you will fail in their practice, and undermine their purpose.

So how should you engage this prayer journey? St. Ignatius wanted people with generous hearts who were aware that they needed God's help.

✠ Jesus proclaimed that the sick needed a Physician, not the well (Mk 2:17). We are all sick and only those willing to see their spiritual ills will submit to the Divine Physician's healing embrace in the Whole-Life Confession journey. If you know you are ill, and believe you *cannot* get better without God's help, welcome.

✠ Jesus calmed the storm that terrified His disciples (Mk 5:35-41). Engage the Whole-Life Confession journey if you are distressed about the chaos in your life and believe God is calling you to a secure shore.

✠ Jesus can heal chronic illness, but He has come to forgive us our sins, and open to us eternal life (Lk 5:17-26). Engage in the Whole-Life Confession journey if you want to experience Jesus' power to forgive your sins.

✠ Jesus encouraged John the Baptist and his followers not to take offense at Him when their faith in Christ brought them suffering and threats (Mt 5:2-6). Engage the Whole-Life Confession journey if the practice of your faith is causing you to suffer persecution for Christ's sake. Hold fast to belief in Him as the Son of God and take no offense.

✠ Jesus invited the weary and the overburdened to find rest in Him (Mt 11:25-30). Engage the Whole-Life Confession journey if you are weary with your life and find yourself overburdened.

✠ Jesus invited the rich young man to surrender his possessions and follow Him (Mk 10:17-25). Engage the Whole-Life Confession journey if you are ready to let go of what is holding you down, and are willing to follow a new path.

✠ Jesus invited Zacchaeus to come down from his tree and follow Him home (Lk 19:1-10). Engage the Whole-Life Confession journey if your privilege, position and places of honor have not brought you the peace, security and hope they promised.

✠ Jesus invited the woman of Samaria to drink the living water that wells up to eternal life (Jn 4:4-42). Engage the Whole-Life Confession journey if you are ready to surrender the cynicism of failed love and relationships, are ready to forgive, and ready to move forward with your life.

✠   Jesus chided the work-anxious Martha to allow Mary to sit at His feet (Lk 10:38-42). Engage with the Whole-Life Confession journey if you are ready to sit still awhile, each day, and listen to the Kingdom within.

✠   Jesus invited Peter to join Him in His work (Lk 5:10-11). Engage the Whole-Life Confession journey if you trust that your sins, addictions and failures do not limit Jesus' desire to take your hand in discipleship as He writes your *Sacred Story*.

✠   Jesus demanded to know the names of the Gerasene's demons (Mk 5:1 20). Engage the Whole-Life Confession journey if you are weary of your spiritual, psychological, and material demons. Welcome the Whole-Life Confession journey if you are willing to name them, with Jesus by your side, and allow Him to deliver you and heal the spiritual and psychic darkness—the habits, sins, and addictions—that rob you of freedom and peace.

✠   God invited the Blessed Virgin Mary not to fear but to say *yes* and participate in the eternal plan of salvation (Lk 1:26-38). Engage the Whole-Life Confession journey if you are ready to let your heart be Christ's home and so labor with Him for universal reconciliation.

✠   Jesus invited His disciples to dine with Him (Jn 15:1-17). Enter the Whole-Life Confession journey if you desire unbounded love, joy, and peace 'share in (Christ's) his sufferings so that (you) we may share in His glory.'"

✠   Jesus invited anyone wishing to follow Him to deny themselves, pick up their cross daily, and follow Him (Lk 9:23). Engage the Whole-Life Confession journey if you can *willingly* allow Christ to reveal your narcissism and by His grace, transform your life into *Sacred Story*.

✠   Jesus invited His disciples to keep a vigilant heart, to reject carousing and drunkenness, and to avoid getting trapped in the anxieties of life, lest they be surprised on the day of the Son of Man (Lk

21:34-36). Engage the Whole-Life Confession journey if today is your day to hearken to the Son of Man, and to return to God with all your heart.

03

Preparation Day 2

Welcome to your second preparation day for your spiritual journey. For your spiritual exercise day two preparation, we will take the time necessary to prayerfully and reflectively read one of the four Gospels. Many of us have never taken the time to listen to Jesus' story by reading, prayerfully from start to finish, one of the four accounts left for us by the early followers. Only read one of the Gospels, but read it reflectively and prayerfully in a place of restful solitude. This place can be at home or some other favorite place you love to be alone in peace and quiet. Perhaps it will be your place of prayer for these next 4 weeks to allow Jesus to reveal your *Sacred Story.* Which Gospel should you read?

--**St. Matthew** writes to convince the Jews that Jesus is indeed the promised Messiah, the Davidic King, foretold by the prophets.

--**St. Mark** reveals Jesus as the true Son of God who suffered and died to achieve complete victory over sickness, sin and death.

--**St. Luke**, the physician, writes to reveal Jesus as the promise and hope of the poor and the weak.

--**St. John,** the mystic, reveals Jesus as the Logos, the Word of God, who with the Father, pre-existed creation and is the One who will save us.

Read the Gospel that immediately speaks to your heart at this time in your life. Don't rush your reading of the Gospel. There is no hurry. Relish The Story of the One who created you and through his birth, life, passion, death and resurrection has offered you eternal life through the forgiveness of your sins.

Jesus is real and wants to become part of your daily life. He wants a relationship with you. He waits to be your hope, your forgiveness and your peace. Open your heart to Him as you read His SACRED STORY.

ೞ

Preparation Day 3

Sacred Story Affirmations

Welcome to your third preparation day for your spiritual journey. For day three of your preparation to enter the Whole-Life Confession journey, listen to the *Affirmations.* They sketch most of the realities you will encounter in your spiritual journey with *Whole-Life Confession* journey.

As your first spiritual disciplines of this process, take some days to reflectively contemplate these *Affirmations* for your *Sacred Story* practice. Use your 15-minute *Sacred Story* prayer times for this purpose. Take as many days as you desire and listen attentively to them. Do not limit the number of days or sessions you spend with them. Your heart, by its peacefulness, will lead you forward to the next exercises at the right time. Trust God's grace working in your heart to lead you.

As you listen to *Sacred Story Affirmations*, be attentive to all the persons, events and issues in your life. Be especially attentive to the things that cause fear, stress, anxiety, anger or grief. When these feelings/emotions surface, notice *how* and *if* they connect with the *Affirmations* that you are contemplating. Always listen with your mind in your heart to the events, issues and persons in your life story. Be curious. Listen to how or why these events, issues, and persons may be linked to the spiritual, emotional and moral dimension of your experiences. Again, pay particular attention to those that might stimulate grief, anxiety, stress, anger and fear.

The Whole-Life Confession focuses attention on things that are both delightful and difficult to experience. But as St. Ignatius learned, focusing attention on the difficult things is very fruitful. These aspects of your life history have the potential to rob you of hope, joy, love, and freedom. You can experience deeper, lasting peace by letting difficulties arise and allowing the Divine Physician to heal you. We have nothing to fear with Christ by our side. Take as long as you desire today to reflect on the *Affirmations* of your *Sacred Story*. Come back to them often in your four-week journey to Christ in your *Whole-Life Confession.*

Sacred Story Affirmations

My *Sacred Story* takes a lifetime to write.

Be Not Afraid!
Fear comes from the enemy of my human nature.

The pathway to God's peace and healing runs through my heart's brokenness, sin, fear, anger and grief.

God resolves all my problems with time and patience.

℘

I will have difficulties in this life.

There are just two ways to cope with my difficulties.
One leads to life, one to death. I will choose life.

℘

"Impossible" is not a word in God's vocabulary.

The *Whole-Life Confession* leads to my freedom and authenticity, but does not always make me feel happy.
℘

My life's greatest tragedies can be transformed
into my life's major blessings.

Times of peace and hope always give way to times of difficulty and stress.

Times of difficulty and stress always give way to times of peace and hope.

છ

I will not tire of asking God for help
since God delights in my asking.

The urge to stop the *Whole-Life Confession* journey

always comes before my greatest breakthroughs.

છ

God gives me insights, not because I am better than others,
but because I am loved.

The insights and graces I need to move forward in life's journey
unfold at the right time.

છ

My personal engagement with the *Whole-Life Confession* accomplishes,
through Christ, a work of eternal significance.

Inspirations can have a divine or a demonic source. I pray for the grace
to remember how to discern one from the other.

છ

Christ, who has walked before me, shares my every burden.
Christ, who has walked before me, will help me resolve every crisis.
Christ, who has walked before me, knows my every hope.

THE WHOLE-LIFE CONFESSION

Christ, who has walked before me, knows everything I suffer.

Christ, who walks before me, will always lead me home to safety.

&

I will strive to curb temptations to react to people and events.
I will ask myself what causes my anger and irritation
at people and events.
I will seek to identify the source of my anger and irritation.
I will give thanks for what angers and upsets me;
for Identifying their source will help to set me free.

I will strive to listen, watch and pray; listen, watch and pray.
I will listen, watch and pray!

&

Everyone has been mortally wounded spiritually, psychologically, and
physically by Original Sin and the loss of paradise.

Journeying with Christ to the roots of my sins and addictions
will help break their grip.

I will not waste time worrying about my sins and failures.
I will use my time wisely and ask God to help me
understand the source of my sins and failings .
I will trust that Christ came to heal all my wounds.

&

Christ's ability to transform my life into a Sacred Story is related to
my openness to His grace.
The process begins when I ask for the grace to
honestly name my sins and addictions.

The process continues when I invite Christ to illuminate my narcissism.
Only God's grace and mercy can write my *Sacred Story*.

&

I will strive daily to pick up the cross, for it leads to my life.

The closer I get to holiness, the more I will see and feel
sin's disorder in my life.

The more I experience sin's disorder, the more tempted I will
be to disbelieve my life as *Sacred Story*.

The way through the temptation is to surrender
my powerlessness to God.

&

It is never too late to open my heart to Christ
and live my life as *Sacred Story*.
Christ, who is close to the brokenhearted, restores my lost innocence.

The path to my *Sacred Story* is
in accepting the healing and forgiveness of
the Divine Physician every day of my life.

&

Your heart is prepared and you have awakened to the path you are
to take. Trust it. Remember: Do not read ahead. Do not exercise ahead.
Awaken to the present moment. Take each day, and each exercise as it
comes.

The Whole-Life Confession begins a Relationship that will carry me

for the rest of my life.
I will learn the fundamentals and strive to
open my heart to God.

I trust that God will lead me.

I believe that my *Whole-Life Confession* will unfold in truth,
in powerlessness and with my patience.

I believe that Jesus awaits me with His grace, mercy and forgiving love.

What do I need for this journey?
a generous heart;
the willingness to take 20-minutes to pray daily
and the humility to always ask God for help.

℘

Week 1

FIRST

Welcome to week one of your spiritual journey. I will choose a place of contemplative rest and reflection. It will be a place apart—a technology-free zone! I will make a decision where to make my spiritual exercise prayer breaks each day. Regularity is the key to sustainable disciplines of any kind, and is especially true of this prayer relationship with Christ.

SECOND

If there are no specific journal assignments for a given day this week, spend two minutes at the end of the exercise and write a short response to each of these two questions: (by "short" we mean ½ to 2 sentences max—no more!)
1) What in the spiritual exercise today increased my faith, hope and love? Be specific and brief.
2) What in the spiritual exercise today decreased my faith, hope and love. Be specific but brief.

THIRD

I will take my 20-minute quiet moments to do the week's exercises. Set your heart to the path you are to take. Trust it. The path leading to Christ in the *Sacred Story* practice has some simple Rules that will help you immensely.

Say this litany aloud before each prayer session this week:

I will not read ahead.

I will awaken to the present moment.

I will take each day and each exercise as it comes.

Be Not Afraid:
Fear comes from the enemy of my human nature.

I cannot do better by going faster.

෩

Day 1

Read this first:

First, say the litany that begins this week.

Welcome to day one of your spiritual journey. You will have a new prayer exercise for every day of this week. Engage the prayers and exercises of the *Whole-Life Confession* with your whole being--with *your mind in your heart.* Be a thinking, reflective "feeler" and believer. Awaken!

Remember, you are a pilgrim, journeying alongside Ignatius himself, in this prayer journey. The Lord Jesus will reward you for your courage and your resolve. Christ promises to be faithful to you! He will help you every possible step of the way because He came, lived and died so you might have abundant life and bear fruit that endures to eternity. Thank Him in advance for the great blessings and insights you will receive. Live today and each day in gratitude to God for all life's blessings and gifts.

ℂ

St. Ignatius and His Legacy - A Fallen Soldier

Until his thirtieth year Ignatius Loyola was unconscious of the sacredness of his life. Instead, he was sincerely devoted to life's pleasures and vanities. He was a gambling addict, sexually self-indulgent, arrogant, hotheaded and insecure. Ignatius' mother died when he was an infant and his father died when he was sixteen.

By our contemporary measures, Ignatius' family was dysfunctional. Was this person a possible candidate for sainthood? It did not look promising. But God does not judge by human standards. It is God's nature to pursue all who have fallen asleep through sin, addiction and selfishness. God judges the heart; with unbounded grace and patient mercy God reaches into the ruins that sin makes of our lives and transforms them into *Sacred Stories*.

Ignatius, with all his narcissism, psychological problems and sinful vices, was awakened by God's great love. A failed military campaign and a shattered leg forced him into a lengthy convalescence back at Loyola castle, his family home. Ignatius' time of recuperation provided an opportunity for Love to shine a light on much more serious and life-threatening wounds that were spiritual, emotional and psychological in nature.

These wounds were supported by the evolution of a destructive, sinful narcissism. For thirty years Ignatius' narcissism had rendered him unconscious to his true human nature and oblivious to his life as *Sacred Story*. The pleasures he indulged in and the power he wielded functioned like a narcotic to numb the pain of his hidden spiritual and psychological wounds. His sinful vices and self-indulgent pleasures blinded him to his authentic human nature and a fruitful life guided by a well-formed conscience.

God's grace reached into the reality of Ignatius' life and awakened in him a desire for innocence. His long-buried aspirations for living authentically suddenly became his prime motivation. He noticed it first while convalescing at Loyola. He became aware of new desires and a different energy while he daydreamed in reading stories of Christ and the saints. Pondering the saints' lives he imagined himself living a different, selfless life.

He compared these new daydreams to his usual vain, narcissistic daydreams. The old daydreams drew energy from a life of sin, addiction and vice while the daydreams of selfless generosity produced their own energy. Ignatius noticed a significant difference between the two sets of daydreams and the feelings they produced. The vain fantasies entertained him when he was thinking about them. But he noticed that when he set them aside, he felt empty and unsatisfied.

A graced experience of God's love opened Ignatius to: → ↓	GIVE THANKS FOR FAVORS RECEIVED ↓
A dissatisfaction with vain fantasies which led to surrendering to holy daydreams, characterized by consolation, which in turn: → ↓	PRAY FOR GRACE TO SEE CLEARLY ↓
Caused him to review his life and actions leading to: → ↓	GIVE A DETAILED ACCOUNT OF CONSCIENCE: GENERAL AND PARTICULAR ↓
Grief with yearning for penance and repentance for his past sins, culminating in: → ↓	ASK PARDON FOR ONE'S FAULTS ↓
Ignatius' passion to amend his life and a desire to love God wholeheartedly. →	RESOLVE AND AMEND TO SERVE GOD

The new holy daydreams also entertained him when he was thinking about them. Yet when he set these aside, he remained content and felt an enduring calm and quiet joy. By paying close attention to the ultimate affective results of these two sets of daydreams and discerning their difference, Ignatius made a discovery that transformed his life and the history of Christian spirituality.

ᦕ

Day 2

Read this first:

First, say the litany that begins this week.

Welcome to day two of your spiritual journey. Your goal is to listen to Ignatius' story and be attentive to any issues that seem important to you. *Listen* to Ignatius' story and pay attention to whatever stirs in you, be it hope and peace or anxiety and fear. Doing this sharpens your spiritual radar for things that make your heart say: "Pay Attention!" Thank Christ in advance for the blessings and insights you will receive.

ॐ

St. Ignatius and His Legacy - The Voice of Conscience

Ignatius discovered that the new, selfless aspirations were influenced by Divine inspirations. He further discovered that these inspirations reflected his true human nature and that the vain fantasies deadened his conscience. His narcissistic daydreams led him away from enduring peace because they masked his authentic human nature. The old daydreams were powerful, ego affirming, and familiar.

He knew in his heart that living their fantasy was the path to self-destruction. On the one hand he would be judged successful by the standards of the world, a world that measured success in terms of riches, honors, and pride.

On the other hand, he would be judged a failure by the standards of the Gospel, standards that advocated a life of spiritual poverty, humility and consequential service—a *Sacred Story* that endures to eternal life.

Ignatius was awakened to the emotional wisdom and spiritual truth of his new daydreams. He became aware of the significant damage that his old lifestyle had done to both himself and others. What had been awakened in him was the divine gift of conscience, and with it, Ignatius experienced profound regret and sorrow for having wasted so much of his life on self-indulgent pleasures and fantasies, seductions that could never bring him lasting peace and satisfaction. He began to understand that living in pleasure and fantasy destroyed his authentic human nature and silenced his deepest desires.

Divine inspiration inspired Ignatius to seek forgiveness for wasting his life and abusing his innocence. Grace enabled Ignatius to take responsibility for his sins against God and his authentic human nature.

Divine inspiration provided Ignatius with the desire, energy, and courage to renounce the thoughts, words, and deeds of his sinful habits. Grace, received through the Sacrament of Reconciliation, heightened Ignatius' consciousness and enabled him to imagine a new path for his life, and new ways to express his gifts and talents.

As usually happens when people respond to the grace of conversion, Ignatius' new aspirations confused and disconcerted many of his closest family members and friends.

Nonetheless he acted on these aspirations. Ignatius was now able to understand a path to God, a *pattern of conversion* that countless thousands would imitate.

CS

Day 3

Read this first:

First, say the litany that begins this week.

Welcome to day three of your spiritual journey. Your goal is to listen to Ignatius' story and be attentive to any issues that seem important to you. *Listen* to Ignatius' story and pay attention to whatever stirs in you, be it hope and peace or anxiety and fear. Doing this sharpens your spiritual radar for things that make your heart say: "Pay Attention!" Thank Christ in advance for the blessings and insights you will receive.

∞

St. Ignatius and His Legacy - A Menacing Fear Unmasked

After some months of living in the light of these new positive virtues, habits, and Divine inspirations, Ignatius was suddenly gripped by terror and panic. How could he manage to live the rest of his life without the pleasures of the past? It was easy to live virtuously for some months, but for the rest of his life? This was a real crisis because Ignatius began to wonder if this was an impossible goal.

Ignatius had two vital insights about this menacing fear. First, he realized it was a counter-inspiration prompted by the *enemy of his true human nature*. The panicky fear led him to think that it would be impossible to live virtuously for such a long time.

Second, the counter-inspiration tempted him to return to his old narcissistic vices and habits. Seduced by their powerful influence, Ignatius would abandon all hope for a life of virtue. In essence, Ignatius was tempted to surrender living the authentic life that had finally brought him peace. He sensed an evil source inspiring this menacing fear and he challenged it head-on: "You pitiful thing! Can you even promise me one hour of life?"

A Decisive and Enduring Commitment to Remain Awake

Not knowing how he would endure, Ignatius dismissed the counter-inspiration and its evil author by re-committing to this new wakefulness for the remainder of his life. This was Ignatius' second insight: NEVER trust the messages prompted by menacing fears.

A enemy voice evokes Ignatius' fear of a lifelong struggle with his sinful habits. → ↓	CONSCIOUS FEAR AND ANXIETY OVER SURRENDERING SINFUL AND ADDICTIVE HABITS ↓
Ignatius rejects the "enemy of human nature" and confronts his false promises. → ↓	CONFRONTING THE THREATENING "VOICE" OF SIN AND ADDICTION WITH THE "TRUTH" THAT THEY BRING DEATH, NOT LIFE ↓
Peace is restored after truthfully naming sin and addiction as death dealing. →	PEACE RETURNS AND ANXIETY DISSOLVES

Counter them with a firm commitment to stay the course, to awaken and remain conscious. This decisive, enduring commitment to persevere restored tranquility, and his fear abated. Ignatius had discovered, unmasked and confronted the deceiver. In this Ignatius learned another lesson about speaking truth to power that would guide his new life and help shape his first set of foundational discernment principles.

Ignatius had to face these same fears many, many more times. Eventually he knew they were false fears, *inspirations* of the enemy of his human nature. Most importantly, he gradually learned how to diffuse them, and to defend against them.

It is vital that we understand this lesson from Ignatius: anyone who changes his or her lifestyle through a Divine awakening and who, by grace, consciously and consistently enters his or her *Sacred Story*, will encounter the same menacing fears.

You can be strongly tempted to fall asleep and slip back into old habits and vices. When you are faced with these menacing fears—*when*, not *if*—confidently recommit to the path of life, and to the Author of life. The fears, in time, will subside. The enemy of human nature will always be disarmed.

Our spirit, body and God's grace at work in us compose a holy trinity. God made us this way. All three parts working cooperatively are necessary for holiness and human growth. In the paradise depicted in Genesis, the perfect cooperation of this trinity of human nature rendered us immortal.

By turning from the fullness of God's grace, our immortality was lost: the perfect balance of the Divinely crafted trinity of human nature— body, spirit and God's grace—shattered. Christ's incarnation and death opened the way to immortality once again.

Our Christian life is a labor of love. In order for God's love to heal us we must do our part to open ourselves to God's graces. This requires conscious and ongoing effort to abstain from sinful, addictive habits in thoughts, words and deeds. There is a need to pray for God's grace. First we must awaken to that grace.

With that same grace, we have the strength to resist and abstain from sinful, addictive attitudes and behaviors, both spiritual and material. God's grace infuses our spiritual disciplines, activating the trinity of our human nature. Grace helps us climb out of the spiritual, mental physical and emotional ruts of our bound self. In doing so, God graces us with a future of increased hope holiness and balance.

CB

Day 4

Read this first

First, say the litany that begins this week.

Welcome to day four of your spiritual journey. The exercises continue with the conversion story of St. Ignatius. As you listen to St. Ignatius' history, reflect on your own. As you read, recall that Ignatius woke up to the fact that there were two plots in his daydreams:

Plot "A" entailed the goals and fantasies rooted in his wounded heart and following narcissistic dreams.

Plot "B" entailed fantasies of a heart rooted in Christ and discovering healing and peace by following holy dreams.

You are invited to search your own daydreams and fantasies for signs of these two plots. Consider your life as you listen to Ignatius' story. God used him to guide us. Each person has the same challenge of finding the narrow path that leads to our true human nature.

∞

St. Ignatius and His Legacy - A Journey to the Heart- Ignatius in Control

Ignatius' decisive and enduring commitment to his conversion launched him directly into the center of his heart's brokenness and the pride masking those wounds. After leaving home Ignatius traveled to Montserrat and spent three days reviewing his life. It was at this time that he made a general confession of all his past sinful deeds. This first life confession initiated an enduring habit of weekly confession and communion. In this written confession Ignatius consciously detailed his sinful attitudes, behaviors and passions: gambling addiction, sexual self-indulgence, arrogance, and violent outbursts of temper. It took all three days to write the story of his past life.

Yet he discovered that simply detailing and confessing his sinful habits and addictions did not disarm them. That would require going deeper, to their source in his heart and history. Only in these deepest recesses could he confront the pattern of spiritual and psychological dysfunction that was most responsible for eroding his freedom and distorting his authentic human nature.

It is this inward journey that fully awakened his conscience. It was only at this depth that he discovered his authentic human nature and regained the creativity of childlike innocence. We do well to understand the tipping point of Ignatius' life from his root vices and narcissism to his new life of wakefulness, light, peace and hope. This is how his story unfolded.

Ignatius' new, pious habit of regular confession evolved into a destructive obsessive and compulsive torture. He confessed and re-confessed past sins multiple times, never feeling he had gotten to the bottom of his immoral deeds. This excruciating spiritual and psychological torment lasted for months. He was so anguished by his obsessive guilt that numerous times he wanted to commit suicide by throwing himself off the cliff where he prayed.

Well aware of the emotional damage caused by this obsessive confession habit, he still could not let it go. Instead he initiated new, harsher physical disciplines and spiritual regimens. His goal was to gain complete control and self-mastery over his immoral and dissolute past. He wanted to remember every detail of his past sins so he could be perfectly cleansed. But nothing worked!

Finally, exhausted and disgusted with his efforts, he realized he intensely despised the spiritual life he was living. Ignatius had an urgent and compelling desire to "stop it!" This thought alarmed Ignatius, and his spiritual radar went on high alert. Ignatius discerned the inspiration came from another source but what could it be?

He discovered the inspiration's origin and author only by understanding where the inspiration was taking him. It occurred to him that the inspiration was leading him in the same direction as the menacing fear he had previously experienced. Inspired to abandon his newly awakened life, Ignatius was being tempted to abandon the peace, the service to others, and the virtuous life of his *Sacred Story*.

But *how* did this counter-inspiration succeed in gaining control? Ignatius' decision to stop re-confessing his past sins reveals the enemy's strategy.

Surrendering Control to Embrace Powerlessness & Innocence

Ignatius' decision to stop his damaging confession habit appears inconsequential. But the choice was the most significant spiritual decision in his entire life. It was also the most difficult, because that one choice meant fully surrendering his life to God. It meant admitting his powerlessness over his sins and in humility allowing God, not himself, to be the source of his holiness.

Reflecting on the temptation to walk away from his new Christian life, Ignatius received an insight that the burdensome, destructive habit of re-confessing past sins was rooted in a pride to try and save himself. This pride forced him to his knees. On seeing this he "awoke as if from a dream," and was given the grace to stop the habit.

Looking at his life spiritually and psychologically, it appears that behind the sexual misdeeds, addictive gambling, and violent temper, there was a controlling, narcissistic pride and a broken heart.

Our narcissistic control is solidified by the searing spiritual and psychological pain of lost innocence: the pattern of sins we inherit from the Original Sin, along with those sins committed against us early in life, and later those sins committed by us.

Our narcissism, if you will, *godifies* us, severely restricting our ability to respond to the true God. We fill the void of our wounded, broken hearts with self-centered strivings for attention, power and control. It is a false identity, an anti-story. Our narcissism blinds us to our authentic human nature and the deepest desires of our heart. It blinds us to our *Sacred Story*.

Ignatius' first life confession at Montserrat documented the *visible* manifestations of this deep distortion in his human nature. The Divine Physician next led Ignatius to the source of those visible sins. It was his wounded human nature that fueled the controlling, narcissistic personality.

The pattern of *visible* sins, vices and addictions was only the tip of the iceberg. It is vital to remember that Ignatius' weaning from the narcotics of aggression, addictions, and dissoluteness opened a portal to his broken heart—his wounded human nature—where he could fully confront his powerlessness and brokenness.

It is here that he finally meets Christ face to face. It is here, in accepting Christ's forgiveness, that healing love begins. It is here that Ignatius admits his powerlessness to save himself and surrenders control of his life to God. This is the spiritual paradigm of powerlessness.

Ignatius' struggle with the obsessive habit of re-confessing past sins was the *symbol* of his *hidden* root sin of pride. Christ labored hard to meet Ignatius right where he was, in this harrowing place. Ignatius' frenzied, damaging re-confessing of past sins was only the latest manifestation of the same hidden narcissism that distorted his first thirty years of life.

The same sin was in full view on the battlefield at Pamplona when Ignatius forced his will on the commander and all the other knights, to engage a suicide mission against a far more numerous and well-armed militia. Ignatius' pride earned him a shattering defeat and a shattered leg. Fortunately his defensive pride was shattered by God's grace awakening him "as if from a dream."

From that moment of surrender at Manresa, Ignatius acknowledged his powerlessness and surrendered control of his life to God. Since Ignatius was very young, God had waited to transform his deepest desires into a *Sacred Story* whose legacy would endure to eternity. This *surrender* defines Ignatius' second set of foundation discernment principles that are at the end of today's lesson

An outpouring of mystical grace flooded Ignatius at this point. More importantly a humble and obedient spirit was beginning to emerge which enabled him to respond to the slightest movements of God's grace in his thoughts, words and deeds. In this humility and docility he discovered a life of service that changed the Church and the world. Later in life he reflected:

There are very few who realize what God would make of them if they abandoned themselves entirely to His hands, and let themselves be formed by His grace. A thick and shapeless tree trunk would never believe that it could become a statue, admired as a miracle of sculpture...and would never consent to submit itself to the chisel of the sculptor who, as St. Augustine says, sees by his genius what he can make of it. Many people who, we see, now scarcely live as Christians, do not understand that they could become saints, if they would let themselves be formed by the grace of God, if they did not ruin His plans by resisting the work which He wants to do.

The proud narcissist, the man who was master of his own universe, became a humble and obedient servant of the universe's true Master and Creator. To arrive at this point, Ignatius had to admit his powerlessness. He had to surrender control over his life and the distorted aspects of his human nature that had evolved over the years. He had to learn how to live out of his newly emerging authentic self, his *true* and free human nature, a true nature that was hidden behind his wounded heart.

Because of this, Ignatius had to also learn how to dismantle the narcissism that had evolved over the first thirty years of his life. The counter-inspirer, the enemy of his human nature, had cleverly concealed his true human nature and Ignatius had to begin life over again, this time allowing God to reveal his authentic self.

This was why, after the resolution of this greatest of his life's crises, Ignatius experienced himself being taught by God. It was, he said, exactly like "a child is taught by a schoolmaster."

‷

Ignatius' struggle with scruples hiding his vainglory ↓ →	The initial confrontation with one's root sin ↓
Ignatius' constant re-confessing to seek salvation by willpower alone ↓ →	The effort to control one's root sin ONLY by personal effort or force of will ↓
Ignatius' suicidal impulses, disgust and the desire to walk away from his new found faith ↓ →	Despair and desire to give up faith when human effort alone fails ↓
Ignatius' tracing the spirit of disgust to a demonic source ↓ →	Insight that desire to reject the spiritual journey is a temptation ↓
Ignatius abandoning his compulsive confessing of past sins →	Admitting powerlessness to save oneself and surrendering prideful actions

Day 5

Read this first:

First, say the litany that begins this week.

Welcome to day five of your spiritual journey. Your goal is to listen to Ignatius' story and be attentive to any issues that seem important to you. *Listen* to Ignatius' story and pay attention to whatever stirs in you, be it hope and peace or anxiety and fear. Doing this sharpens your spiritual radar for things that make your heart say: "Pay Attention!" Thank Christ in advance for the blessings and insights you will receive.

∞

St. Ignatius and His Legacy - The Divine-Inspirer & the counter-inspirer

This harrowing crisis taught Ignatius a most vital lesson about counter-inspirations. The willpower and resolute commitment to live virtuously for the rest of his life could be manipulated and turned against him by means of subtle *inspirations*. What seemed like a holy, pious, and noble practice—a serious approach to confession—devolved into a damaging habit that made him loathe his spiritual life, and in frustration, *inspired* him to abandon it.

He learned that the counter-inspirations of the enemy of his human nature could act like "an angel of light." These inspirations appear holy but when followed, they end in disaster, distancing one from God and from one's authentic self.

Ignatius gained clearer knowledge of the two spiritual forces that inspire and seek to guide the evolution of one's *story*. Ignatius gathered what he had learned from "speaking truth to power" to the enemy of human nature, and what he had learned from surrendering control of his life to God, into guidelines for discerning these different inspirations. For now

43

it is sufficient to say that the Divine-Inspirer is the author of one's *original innocence*, that is, one's authentic and free human nature. The Divine-Inspirer works gently in and through every situation, especially the misfortunes associated with the damaging spiritual and psychological ordeals of life.

It is the nature of the Holy Spirit to offer forgiveness and provide shelter from the enemy of human nature whose sole purpose is to destroy innocence. The Divine-Inspirer forgives sins, restores lost innocence, mends broken and wounded hearts, releases captives, sets the oppressed free, and illumines one's *Sacred Story* and true human nature (Lk 4:18).

The counter-inspirer works through all the events of one's life and relationships. His work is evident in the distortions of spirit and mind, the deep wounding caused by the evolution of sin from the Original Sin and also sin inherited from one's family and culture. The counter-inspirer works to corrupt innocence and deform one's spiritual, emotional, physical and psychological nature—one's *true* human nature.

Jesus condemned the violation of the innocent and the child-like. No human being can escape the machinations this evil breeds in one's body, mind and spirit. Since the Original Sin, this evolutionary force has infected every person and consequently all of human history.

The counter-inspirer conceals our original wounds, counseling and guiding our steps to build a false identity, an anti-story, characteristically identified by a distorted ego and defended by narcissism. Our narcissistic pride rationalizes the habits, vices, addictions and lifestyles that form our anti-story. The counter-inspirer renders us unconscious to our *Sacred Story* and to our true Divinely shaped human nature.

God led Ignatius through this distorted evolution back to the lost innocence of his true human nature. To get there Ignatius had to confront his pattern of spiritual and psychological distortions signified by his narcissistic pride. It was a mighty castle that he had built on the shifting sands of a child's wounded innocence, on a child's lonely, broken heart. God provided Ignatius the inspiration and grace to allow that castle to crumble. The shattering of his powerful defenses and the unmasking of his prideful, narcissistic pattern proved to be the tipping point of Ignatius' entire conversion process.

Wakefulness, Holiness and Heightened Consciousness

Ignatius' conversion from his anti-story and his full awakening to his *Sacred Story* was not a single event but rather a gradual process. His full evolution from a vain egomaniac to a saint took the rest of his life. This is evident in his *Autobiography*. In three linked narratives recounting personal near-death experiences, Ignatius reveals his growth in holiness, a process that evolved over a long, twenty-eight-year period.

In the first account he is filled with fear of judgment because he understands that pride is still a strong temptation for him. In the second account he is no longer afraid of death but instead, he is filled with sorrow for his delayed response to God.

In the third account, grace floods his heart and he is filled with an intense devotion and desire for eternal union with God. These three episodes mirror the three classical stages of mystical growth: purgation, illumination and union. The three episodes also convey the reality of Ignatius' patience with the process of his spiritual growth:

Ignatius, justifying himself, anxiously recoils and focuses on his sinfulness → ↓	Panic over one's salvation due to weakness and sinfulness →	PURGATION ↓
Ignatius, no longer fearful, regrets not having responded sooner to God's graces → ↓	Sadness at slowness of one's response to God's love and invitation to intimacy →	ILLUMINATION ↓
Ignatius' intense joy at the thought of dying and being with God →	An ardent, all-embracing love of God and desire for complete union with the Trinity →	UNION

A Life-Long Commitment to Christ in the Church

It took Ignatius the remainder of his life to develop into the saint we know today. His was a gradual, steady evolution from a sinful narcissist in control of his own life to an innocent, obedient servant of God. He discovered and embraced the power and energy of living in the holy trinity of his authentic human nature—spirit, body and God's grace working in unison.

Growth in holiness requires desire, patience and daily effort to awaken to our authentic human nature. It takes time for grace to penetrate the influence of our anti-story so that our *Sacred Story* can more fully emerge. There are no short cuts to holiness, not even for saints.

If you desire to surrender your anti-story and open to your *Sacred Story*, grace will awaken you, like Ignatius, to places in your heart's memories you might not wish to visit. The awakening will begin like Ignatius'. It starts with an honest identification of the *visible* manifestations of those spiritual and psychological distortions in the particulars of your human nature.

These distortions disclose your lost innocence and a heart broken by the Original Fall and the cumulative sins of your family, clan and culture. Ignatius started this process with his life confession. He truthfully identified the habits, addictions, sins and compulsions characteristic of his lost innocence and broken heart.

Open yourself to the graces of God that will illumine the distinctive narcissistic elements fueling your sinful, compulsive behaviors. Ignatius needed much grace to overcome his defenses and unlock this hidden truth about his life. Everyone who embraces this invitation to walk this path can confidently rely on the same grace to navigate this vital part of the process.

Finally awakening to your *Sacred Story* will take you to the places in your heart where your innocence is wounded, your true human nature is distorted, and your heart is broken. Awakening to your *Sacred Story* will reveal the outlines of your anti-story.

You will need to honestly evaluate the narcissistic pattern in your own life, identifying the pleasures, powers, and habits that act as narcotics, blocking the pain of your broken heart and lost innocence.

This pattern that masks your authentic self and your true human nature is the pattern of your false self. It is the deceit of the anti-story that hides the radiance of your authentic human nature and the sacredness of your life story. This was Ignatius' experience. By divine inspiration he discovered his false-self masquerading as a pious, conscientious penitent.

Once he reached this point, Ignatius awakened, "as if from a dream," to his *Sacred Story*. By so doing, he was graced to unite mind and spirit, action and contemplation, the eternal in the present moment, and so to see the Divine Presence in all people and in all creation.

His new consciousness of God so energized him that he could daily enter the stream of his *Sacred Story*, enabling him to reengage life's duties and obligations with a serene heart and with clarity of purpose. He courageously allowed God to write his *Sacred Story* over the remainder of his life—hourly, daily, weekly, monthly, yearly.

The vitality of Ignatius' personal relationship with God, in Father, Son and Spirit, was possible through the grace and gratitude he experienced in the constant encounter with his personal sinfulness and disordered passions. These graced encounters always brought illumination, insight, energy and hope, never discouragement, fear or despair.

A proud, dissolute, insecure narcissist finally found serenity and security in God's full love, acceptance, mercy, and forgiveness. Interestingly enough, this happened in and through Ignatius' powerlessness and weaknesses and perhaps even because of them! Learn this lesson: the sin and weakness which so marred his early life became the very source of his strength and sanctity. Ignatius discovered, like St. Paul, that in his weaknesses and sin, he was strong in Christ (2 Cor 12:10). It will be the same for you.

CB

Day 6

Read this first

First, say the litany that begins this week.

Welcome to day six of your spiritual journey. The next exercises—days six and seven-- move from the conversion story of St. Ignatius to your own story. You are invited to make a commitment to join with St. Ignatius and all the holy women and men in the Church, to give your life to Christ for this great work of reconciliation.

Listen to the call and pay attention to whatever stirs in you, be it hope and peace or anxiety and fear. Doing this sharpens your spiritual radar for things that prompt your heart to say: "Pay Attention!" Thank Christ in advance for the blessings and insights you will receive.

ℰᴐ

St. Ignatius and His Legacy - The Call to Universal Reconciliation

Your Sacred Story

As with Ignatius, God extends an invitation to awaken to the pattern of spiritual, emotional and psychological dysfunction that has formed our anti-story. God invites us to awaken to our lives as *Sacred Story* and to produce fruit that endures to eternity. The awakening and growth will reveal where our freedom is compromised and how we close our hearts to our authentic human nature.

Christ compassionately shows us how our selfishness and pride have corrupted our creativity, robbing us of the joy of innocence. God's invitation is gentle. God's awakening is merciful. Rest assured that God's passion is to pursue us, rescue us, heal us and bring us back to our original innocence. God's passion is Personal. God's passion is Love. God's passion is Christ Jesus.

God's intention is to gradually heal and transform our thoughts, words and deeds. For every thought, word and deed influences my history in the direction of an anti-story or a *Sacred Story*. Every thought, word and deed, for good or ill, touches all people in my life, the entire world and all of creation, shaping history's final chapter.

The effects of sin and narcissism—as well as the effects of virtue and selflessness—have individual, social, physical, spiritual, and ecological ramifications that reach to the ends of creation. For everything and everyone is one in Love—one in Christ Jesus—through whom and for whom everything was made (Rom 11:36).

Every thought, word, or deed, no matter how discreet, has positive or negative significance in the interconnected web of life that God has fashioned through Christ. It is Christ's being—His *SACRED STORY*—that links each of our individual *Sacred Stories*. It is in Christ that the entire cosmos is joined together. God in Christ has made us responsible for and dependent upon each other and upon the earth that sustains us.

The Christ of the Cosmos—through whom and for whom everything was made—became man, and confronted, absorbed, and diffused all the destructive force of evil's evolutionary anti-history running through human nature and the created cosmos. Christ reconciles in Himself everything in the heavens and on the earth to bring peace to all by the blood of His cross. His *SACRED STORY* redeems and renews every chapter in our history, individual and collective.

Christ Jesus passionately awaits our participation to join His work of universal reconciliation. Our willingness to accept the path of conversion entails truthfully identifying our sins, dysfunction and addictions. It entails experiencing and admitting our powerlessness to save ourselves. It requires the patience of a lifetime while Christ writes our *Sacred Story*.

My participation in Christ's work of reconciliation is the only worthy vocation and the only labor that produces fruit enduring to eternity. My accepting the invitation unlocks the very mystery of life.

When I accept the invitation, Christ promises to share His universal glory. Accepting the invitation to intentionally enter my *Sacred Story* has momentous consequences.

Now Is the Time to Wake from Sleep

Our time on this earth is so very brief. Since the time of Christ's birth, life, death and resurrection, our story can only be measured and valued in light of His eternal mission of Reconciliation. Intentionally entering my *Sacred Story* will, over time, enable me to know God more intimately and serve God more generously.

Like Ignatius, I am called to awaken from sleep—to awaken to wholeness and holiness. I was created and infused with the gift to awaken to a life that reverences the God, who in Christ and the Holy Spirit, is present in all things: all persons, and all creation.

Awakening to my *Sacred Story*, like Ignatius, calls for courage in the cleansing of the spirit and psyche that it initiates. The process requires discipline in the face of temptation and monotony. It requires consciously asking, even begging if necessary, for God's graces. It requires time and patience; deliberately choosing each day to be faithful to time and space for God.

Awakening requires the patience of a lifetime. Embraced and trusted, the journey is rich with blessings beyond our wildest expectations. Encountering Christ daily in *Sacred Story* forever changes life, relationships, the earth, and eternity.

What is needed for the journey will be provided each day. In my journey through the memories and experiences, past and present, I am promised the power and mercy of the LOVE that maintains and guides the entire cosmos. It is this LOVE that waits to transform your sins, addictions, angers, fears, grief, guilt and shame. It is this LOVE that restores your broken heart into a vessel of forgiveness, light and peace.

The more embedded and impenetrable the web of darkness, compulsion, sin, and addiction in your life, the more strategic and magnificent is God's grace in breaking its grip, for nothing is impossible with God (Lk 1:37).

On this journey you will gain personal and real knowledge of sin and mercy, creation and eternity. You will come to know, experientially, our gracious God, present in Christ's Body in the Church, in the sacraments, in yourself, in others, and in all creation. Some of your insights will come in a flash; others will unfold over weeks, months, or years.

From now on the whole process of your life is about waking from sleep (Eph 5:14; Rom 13:11), bending to the real, to the authentic, to your true human nature, living and working for fruit that endures to eternity.

08

Day 7

Read this first

First, say the litany that begins this week.

Welcome to day seven of your spiritual journey. The next exercises—days six and seven-- move from the conversion story of St. Ignatius to your own story. You are invited to make a commitment to join with St. Ignatius and all the holy women and men in the Church, to give your life to Christ for this great work of reconciliation.

Listen to the call and pay attention to whatever stirs in you, be it hope and peace or anxiety and fear. Doing this sharpens your spiritual radar for things that prompt your heart to say: "Pay Attention!" Thank Christ in advance for the blessings and insights you will receive.

℅

St. Ignatius and His Legacy - Your Sacred History

Your life (and each person's life) is inextricably interwoven and integrated to Christ's *SACRED STORY* in ways both mysterious and sublime. It is mysterious because the ways of this world are not the ways of the Kingdom. What is deemed valuable and successful in this present age is in fact foolish and useless in the spiritual life.

It is sublime because the most private sufferings offered to God, the faintest cries for mercy and forgiveness, and the simplest acts of care, kindness or generosity done for one's enemy, God's beloved poor, and His magnificent creation, are written in gold in the Book of the Lamb. These are the thoughts, words, and deeds that will endure to eternity.

There are no short cuts to the story's unfolding. Conversion is lifelong but measurable when I intentionally, daily, consistently, and faithfully enter my *Sacred Story*. My story begins where Ignatius' began, in the grace of the call to conversion. My conversion will begin to take shape when I accept that call and follow the pattern of Ignatius' own conversion. I will discover things that disquiet, create shame and confusion, and unlock hidden angers, fears and grief. I will encounter a heart broken, and innocence and paradise lost.

But most important, in all of this, I will be held, sheltered and guided by the only thing necessary, Christ's love. I will be given strength to speak truth to power. I will be given grace to see and honestly name those sins, habits and addictions that bring death—spiritual, physical, psychological—and not life. Then, surrendering to my powerlessness in favor of God's power, the Divine Physician will rewrite my life as *Sacred Story*.

Surrendering control of my life to the care of the Divine Physician by admitting my powerlessness to save myself will enable me to be vulnerable, creative, innocent, and humble. Once my heart is open, the Spirit of God will continue to write my *Sacred Story.* My lifetime of patience will bear fruit that endures to eternity.

My pilgrim journey, like Ignatius', follows the proven and time-tested mystical path to wholeness and holiness. There are *no* shortcuts. Recall that Christ Jesus Himself has traveled the path. He will guarantee my journey's safe passage and carry my burdens, failures, shame, broken heart, and confusion.

I will hold in my heart the humble example of Jesus washing my feet. He endured humiliations, torture, and a disgraceful death, so that I can find hope and healing for everything in my life that needs healing, forgiveness, and redemption. From the beginning of time His *SACRED STORY* is mystically imprinted into the souls of His chosen people and the Church. Through the pattern of His *STORY*, I, the Church, and all people can have their history rewritten as *Sacred Story.*

I will intentionally enter my life narrative for 15-minute intervals once or twice each day. My story linked to Christ's *SACRED STORY* and to all people and to all creation, runs from my birth in all the thoughts, words and deeds to shape my destiny here, and in the hereafter. The prayer will help me attune to Creation, Presence, Memory, Mercy, and Eternity.

When I encounter the fears, stresses, angers, temptations, failures, addictions and sins in my day, I can briefly attune to Creation, Presence, Memory, Mercy, and Eternity, and ask for the grace to see my whole story. By so doing, the Divine Physician can heal me and awaken my heart to its true human nature.

Christ extends the invitation and His Love, at the Heart of the Universe, awaits my response. I pray for the courage and generosity to enter with Christ into my *Sacred Story*.

ℭℨ

WEEK 1

Optional Meditation

Night Vigil Week 1 [2]

This is the first of four night vigils you can do for your Whole-Life Confession journey. We suggest doing them in an evening and giving the meditation 45-minutes.

NIGHT VIGIL WITH JESUS *Do only one section at a time. Do not read ahead but stay with each section until you feel inclined to move on.*

I. Let yourself be mindful of the presence of Christ Jesus in the Blessed Sacrament. Spend a minute or two to get in a position of prayer that allows you to relax but at the same time stay alert. As you repose in this way, ask God to keep you open to your own life and God's love for the whole retreat. As a way of asking for this grace of openness, pray the *Triple Colloquy* below. Stay with this as long as you are able to remain engaged in this prayer. Move ahead as your heart suggests. Rest with Jesus as his disciples might have at the end of a day of ministry and preaching.

II. "Now it was about this time that he (Jesus) went out into the hills to pray: and he spent the whole night in prayer to God." (Lk. 6:12)

Imagine the kind of place Jesus went to so he could be alone. Spend some time to create in your own imagination the location as you envision it. Pay attention to all things: the color of the evening sky and stars, the rocks and vegetation, the trees and the views from the hills, what the evening air felt like. Place yourself in the scene at a distance from Jesus so he cannot detect your presence. Move on when your heart suggests.

III. After a while, imagine that Jesus notices you alone in that place. Watch as he approaches you and see him sit quietly next to you. He knows you are beginning a journey and after a while he asks you why you have decided to come. What do you say to him as asks you this? Spend some time telling him your hopes and fears. You know he understands what you are saying and the depth of your desires and concerns. The two of you just sit quietly in each other's presence. Stay here for as long as you like. Before you leave the place, ask him for the grace to stay open to what he wants for you to receive from the retreat.

IV. As you walk down the hill, go back to your room slowly praying the words of the *Our Father.*

☙

TRIPLE COLLOQUY OF SAINT IGNATIUS

First Colloquy, or conversation, will be with Mary. Speak with Mary, using your own words, asking her to obtain from her Son the grace to be open to the Spirit working inside you. When you finish this conversation, pray the *Hail Mary* slowly, thinking of the words and the person to whom you are praying.

Hail Mary, full of grace The Lord is with thee.
Blessed art thou amongst women
and blessed is the fruit of thy womb, Jesus.
Holy Mary, Mother of God, Pray for us sinners,
Now and at the hour of our death.
Amen.

Second Colloquy, or conversation, will be with Jesus. Speak directly to Jesus, asking him to request his Father for the same graces as above. When you finish your conversation, pray the *Anima Christi* slowly, thinking of the words and the person to whom you are praying.

Soul of Christ, sanctify me. Body of Christ, save me.
Blood of Christ, fill me. Water from the side of Christ wash me.
Passion of Christ, strengthen me. O Good Jesus, hear me.
Within thy wounds, hide me. Permit me not to be separated from thee.
From the wicked foe, defend me. At the hour of my death, call me,
And bid me come to thee that with thy saints I may praise thee forever
and ever.
Amen.

Third Colloquy, or conversation, will be with God the Father. Ask the Father directly in your own words to give you the graces as described above. When you finish, pray the *Our Father,* thinking of the words and the person to whom you are praying.

Our Father, Who art in heaven Hallowed be thy name.

Thy Kingdom come. Thy will be done, On earth as it is in heaven.
Give us this day our daily bread, And forgive us our trespasses,
As we forgive those who trespass against us.
Lead us not into temptation,
But deliver us from evil.
Amen.

☙

Week 2

FIRST

Welcome to week two of your spiritual journey. I will choose a place of contemplative rest and reflection. It will be a place apart—a technology-free zone! I will make a decision where to make my spiritual exercise prayer breaks each day. Regularity is the key to sustainable disciplines of any kind, and is especially true of this prayer relationship with Christ.

SECOND

If there are no specific journal assignments for a given day this week, spend two minutes at the end of the exercise and write a short response to each of these two questions: (by "short" we mean ½ to 2 sentences max—no more!)
1) What in the spiritual exercise today increased my faith, hope and love? Be specific and brief.
2) What in the spiritual exercise today decreased my faith, hope and love. Be specific but brief.

THIRD

During my prayer exercises this week I will slowly and thoughtfully open my heart to Christ.

Say this litany aloud before each prayer session this week:

THE WHOLE-LIFE CONFESSION

I will ask God to help me.

Be Not Afraid:
Fear comes from the enemy of my human nature.

I will awaken to my spiritual nature

and to the inspirations that inspire faith, hope and love.

I will awaken to persons, events and issues that generate
Faith, Hope or Love - Fear, Anger or Grief.
I will wake up!

I believe that understanding the source of my vices and addictions can
lead to greater joy, authenticity and holiness.

ᚋ

Day 8

Read this first:

First, say the litany that begins this week.

Welcome to day eight of your spiritual journey. Take a moment to ask God for this grace and say this phrase out loud: "Lord, open me to the knowledge of my own heart."

The heart is where the important work of prayer takes place. The mind reveals facts. The heart reveals the truth of my being. The heart is how Scripture describes the most important aspects of the human condition. (Please do not read the Scripture passages below during your exercise but if your heart leads you to read them at some other time, you are encouraged to follow your heart!)

Here are a few examples:

✠ The heart reveals the state of corruption caused by sin (Gen 6:5; Jer 17:9-10; Mt 15:9).

✠ The heart is where the process of conversion and forgiveness takes place (Ez 36:26; Mt 18:35; Rom 2:29).

✠ The heart is the point of convergence, where self-condemnation comes face-to-face with hope in God's power (1 Jn 3:19-20).

✠ The heart's purity enables one to see God (Mt 5:8).

✠ The heart is the locus of compassion (Lk 7:13).

✠ The heart is the custodian of memory and contemplation (Lk 1:29; 2:19, 51).

✠ The heart is the vessel holding the secrets that illuminate the true meaning of life (Mt 6:21; Lk 24:32; Ps 85:9).

✠ The heart is defined as the center of human consciousness and action, wherein God discerns the rightness or wrongness of my thoughts, words, and deeds. The heart is the center from which each person will stand before God and render the ultimate account of their thoughts, words, and deeds (Heb 4:12-13).

✠ The heart perceives love as the ultimate end, gift, and purpose of being (1 Cor 13).

✠ The testimony of Christ in Scripture speaks to the heart's desire for innocence, based on the weariness of life, and the burdens it carries resulting from corruption (Mt 11:28-30.).

✠ Christ also promises to respond to the heart searching for Him, and gives the conviction that He can be found by those who seek Him (Lk 11:9-11).

Seek *knowledge of the heart* and ask God for the grace to open a pathway to your heart. Seek also knowledge of God's heart, present in Christ's Sacred Heart. This grace will help to unite your heart to the heart of Christ. Say it out loud one more time: "Lord, open me to the knowledge of my heart."

Before you end your time of prayer, write one or two sentences and no more, about what knowledge of your heart you would like God to reveal to you. What to do you desire to know? Ask the Lord.

☙

Day 9

Read this first:

First, say the litany that begins this week.

Welcome to day nine of your spiritual journey. Once you are settled in your place of prayer, ask for God's inspiration for this time. Then ask, in words from your heart, to be inspired to discover or remember the most intimate and/or meaningful name for God the Father, Son and Spirit that you have used in prayer.

The name will resonate deeply in your heart and reflect God's relationship to you and your personal relationship with God. The following may be helpful:

Merciful Father, Loving Father, Almighty Father, Our Father, Father God, Loving Creator, Creator God, God of Love, My God, Holy God, Father of the Poor, God of All Mercy, God of All Compassion, Father of Jesus, Lord Jesus Christ, Lord Jesus, Christ Jesus, Dear Jesus, Adorable Jesus, Adorable Christ, Good Jesus, Jesus, Merciful Savior, Jesus My Savior, Son of God, Dearest Lord, My Lord, My Lord and My God, Sacred Heart of Jesus, Lamb of God, Good Shepherd, Crucified Savior, Holy Spirit, Spirit of Jesus, Spirit of the Lord, Loving Spirit, Holy Spirit of God, Love of God, Divine Spirit, Creator Spirit, Creator God.

Ask for the grace to discover the name for God that touches your heart most intimately. You will know the right name because it has the power to unlock your trust and your love, and to stir your affections.

Write the name for God in your notebook when you discover it. From this point forward, use this name when you address God. Speak this name audibly so you can hear yourself say it. God delights when you speak directly from your heart.

Use this name to address God every time you naturally think of God throughout the day. For example, you may say in your heart before a meeting: "Lord Jesus, be with me now." Say it, and then just move on with your meeting.

Do not make this a tedious exercise but one that feels natural and relaxed. You do not have to think long and hard about God. The purpose of this spontaneous prayer is just a short, friendly reminder of God's presence. Use this name if you find yourself conversing with God during the day.

ॐ

Day 10

Read this first:

First, say the litany that begins this week.

Welcome to day ten of your spiritual journey. Review Ignatius' story and your own: Use this question as the focus for these exercises: "Like Ignatius, have I discovered the one area of my life that convinces me, beyond any doubt, that I cannot save myself, and must rely on God to save me?"

Recall the different parts of St. Ignatius' *Sacred Story* narrative. In your prayer time today review the sections of his story that resonate with your own story and recall those parts of his story that moved your heart in one of two ways:

First: What spontaneously evoked *anxiety* in me as I listened to Ignatius' story? I will reflect on why my anxiety was provoked. In my notebook, I will record briefly what evoked my anxiety and why.

Second: As I listened to Ignatius' conversion story, what *inspired* or gave me *hope* about my life? I will reflect on why I was inspired or hopeful. In my notebook I will record briefly what inspired me and why.

CB

Day 11

Read this first:

First, say the litany that begins this week.

Welcome to day eleven of your spiritual journey. You should give yourself permission to make your prayer a little longer today, maybe thirty-minutes, to be inspired and have your memory enlivened.

Each of us has persons, issues and life events that shape our life story, our history. We are conscious of some of these pieces, while others are buried deep in our memory. We seek grace to understand those things that in positive ways shape our thoughts, actions, feelings, and beliefs linked to God, the world and ourselves. These persons, life events and issues are often linked to the spiritual plotlines in our life story, leading towards God.

In this exercise we seek God's grace to awaken to our graced *affective memories*. That is, we want to recall the persons, life events or issues, and *feel* the emotional weight, and the heart value of how they have moved us forward in our history. Because these significant elements often evade our conscious awareness, we need to rely on grace to reveal them.

Naturally, I seek insight into the closest, most intimate circle of people and events in my life story—my parents, family, friends, and important events. I will be attentive to the feeling these memories evoke.

For one person, I might feel mostly love (someone who has cared deeply for me). For another person, I might feel gratitude for how they helped me at one point in my life. For one event I might see God's saving grace.

For another issue, my experience might be gratitude or hope (an issue that has positively transformed my life for the better).

Pray that God enlighten your mind and heart to know each person, issue or life event and the *single, predominant* feeling gratitude, hope or love that each inspires.

છ્ર

So for your spiritual exercise today sit apart in your quiet place. Find a comfortable position that permits you to be alert. Breathe deeply for a few minutes, mindful that God's love sustains your very life.

Next, using the personal name for God you identified last week, ask God to enlighten your memory and imagination so that the most significant people, issues and life events come into your mind and heart.

As you become aware of each, pause briefly and write down the name of the person, or the issue or life event that comes to memory. Next to each of these, write a single word for the most predominant feeling that arises in your heart. A word of caution here: do not succumb to the temptation to analyze or judge the feelings as they arise.

For this exercise, use the following chart to ask God to inspire you to remember the elements (person, issue, or life event) that generate gratitude, hope or love. Pray that those elements *most important* to your history come into your mind and heart.

ෆ

TEN PERSONS/LIFE EVENTS/ISSUES THAT GENERATE

GRATITUDE, HOPE OR LOVE

Person/Life Event/Issue	*Gratitude/Hope/Love*
1.	1.
2.	2.
3.	3.
4.	4.
5.	5.
6.	6.
7.	7.
8.	8.
9.	9.
10.	10.

Day 12

Read this first:

First, say the litany that begins this week.

Welcome to day twelve of your spiritual journey. You should give yourself permission to make your prayer a little longer today, maybe thirty-minutes, to be inspired and have your memory enlivened.

In this exercise we seek God's grace to awaken to our negative *affective memories*. That is, we want to recall the persons, life events or issues, and *feel* the emotional weight, and the heart value of how they have made it difficult to move forward in our history. Because these significant elements often evade our conscious awareness, we need to rely on grace to reveal them.

Naturally, I seek insight into the closest, most intimate circle of people and events in my life story—my parents, family, friends, and important events. I will be attentive to the feeling these memories evoke.

For one life event, I might feel fear (something that has the power to generate the anxiety I know as fear). For another life event, my predominant feeling might be anger (someone or something that hurt me or a loved one). For one issue, my predominant feeling might be grief (the loss of a loved one or an opportunity that grieves my heart).

Pray that God enlighten your mind and heart to know each person, issue or life event and the *single, predominant* feeling (fear, anger, or grief) each inspires.

෯

For your prayer today sit apart in your quiet place. Find a comfortable position that permits you to be alert. Breathe deeply for a few minutes, mindful that God's love sustains your very life.

Next, using the personal name for God you identified last week, ask God to enlighten your memory and imagination so that the most significant people, issues and life events come into your mind and heart.

As you become aware of each, pause briefly and write down the name of the person, or the issue or life event that comes to memory. Next to each of these, write a single word for the most predominant feeling that arises in your heart. Again a word of caution here: do not succumb to the temptation to analyze or judge the feelings as they arise.

For this exercise, use the following chart to ask God to inspire you to remember the elements (person, issue, or life event) that generate fear, anger or grief. Pray that those elements *most important* to your history come into your mind and heart.

CallB

TEN PERSONS/LIFE EVENTS/ISSUES THAT GENERATE

FEAR, ANGER OR GRIEF

Person/Life Event/Issue	*Fear/Anger/Grief*
1.	1.
2.	2.
3.	3.
4.	4.
5.	5.
6.	6.
7.	7.
8.	8.
9.	9.
10.	10.

Day 13

Read this first:

First, say the litany that begins this week.

Welcome to day thirteen of your spiritual journey. You should give yourself permission to make your prayer a little longer today, maybe thirty-minutes, to be inspired and have your memory enlivened.

For this spiritual exercise, pay attention to the vices (Pride, Gluttony, Lust, Sloth, Envy, Avarice, and Anger). These are sometimes called the seven capital sins (from *caput*, the Latin word for *head*) because they are root habits or vices that lead to many other problems. All of us are subject to vices which have the ability to hook us mildly, moderately or strongly.

Simply identlfy your capital sins/vices. Ask Christ, the Divine Physician, to help you understand their **source** and **context** in your life history. Ask for the grace of deeper understanding, and then with Christ, observe your life with compassionate curiosity, and with objectivity. God sees beyond any vices you have, or think you have.

God knows you for who you arc and loves you. Jesus, the Divine Physician, watches compassionately and carried the burden for all your vices. He desires that you gain greater understanding and freedom. He has great compassion and patience for those seeking His help and healing. He wants you to gain insights as to why they are present in your life history so you can find greater hope and freedom.

At the end of each prayer period mark down in your notebook all the capital vices that trap you and to which you are susceptible. Be brief in your writing, but specific. List which capital sins/vices ensnare you and how intensely (mildly, moderately or strongly) they ensnare you.

The Seven Capital Vices

Pride

Pride is an unrestrained and improper appreciation of our own worth. This is listed first because it is widely considered the most serious of the seven sins. Pride—narcissism—was the foundation of Adam and Eve's sin that made them fall for the serpent's temptation "to be like gods." Adam and Eve displaced God, the Creator, as the arbiter of truth and goodness. They, who were creatures, made themselves gods, the final judges of truth and goodness. Their action led to the loss of paradise and to a world of sickness and death. Pride often leads to the committing of other capital sins. Pride is manifest as vanity and narcissism about one's appearance, intelligence, status, wealth, connections, power, successes and all the other things that one uses to stand apart from others and from God.

Greed

Greed is also known as avarice or covetousness. It is the immoderate desire for earthly goods and power. It is a sin of excess. The object of one's greed need not be evil. The problem lies in the way a person regards or desires an object, making it a god and investing it with inappropriate value. Greed can inspire such sinful actions as hoarding, theft, fraud, tax evasion, environmental waste or unethical business practices.

Gluttony

Gluttony comes from the Latin word meaning to gulp down or swallow. It is the sin of over-indulgence and usually refers to over-consumption of food and drink. Gluttony can be eating too soon, too expensively or eating too much. St. Alphonsus Liguori explained that feeling pleasure in eating is not wrong. Because food tastes good, we are delighted by this gift. It is not right however to eat with pleasure as the only motive and to forget food's function in sustaining vitality and health.

Lust

The sin of lust refers to corrupted desires of a sexual nature. Sexuality is a gift from God and pure in itself. However, lust refers to the impure thoughts and actions that misuse that gift. Lust deviates from God's law and sexuality's sacred purpose of allowing woman and man to participate in God's creative nature. Indulging in the sin of lust can include, but is not limited to, fornication, adultery, bestiality, rape, masturbation, pornography and incest.

Sloth

Sloth is often described simply as the sin of laziness. However, while this is part of sloth's character, its true face is spiritual laziness. The sin of sloth means being lazy and lax about living the Faith and practicing virtue. Paraphrasing The Catholic Encyclopedia, sloth means aversion to labor or exertion. As a capital or deadly vice, St. Thomas calls it sadness in the face of some spiritual good that one has to achieve. In other words, a slothful person is bothered by the effort to sustain one's friendship with God. In this sense sloth is directly opposed to charity.

Envy

The sin of envy or jealousy is more than just someone wanting what others have. Sinful envy leads one to emotions or feelings of upset at another's good fortune or blessings. The law of love naturally leads one to rejoice in the good luck of one's neighbor. Envy opposes such love.

Envy is named among the capital sins because of the other sins to which it leads.

Anger

Anger or wrath may be described as excessive and powerful feelings of hatred and resentment. These feelings can manifest as a passionate denial of truths expressed by others. Anger can also manifest in the form of denying truths about one's own life and impatience with the procedure of law. Anger is manifest too, in the desire to seek revenge outside of the workings of the justice system.

Anger, in essence is wishing to do evil or harm to others. The transgressions borne of vengeance are among the most serious, including assault, murder, and in extreme cases, genocide and other crimes against humanity. Anger is the only sin not necessarily associated with selfishness or self-interest, although one can be angry for selfish reasons, such as jealousy.

CB

Day 14

Read this first:

First, say the litany that begins this week.

Welcome to day fourteen of your spiritual journey. For this short spiritual exercise, pay attention to your addictions. Ignatius had addictions to gambling and possibly to sex. Everyone has addictions (whether mild moderate or strong) to one or more things. Our addictions reveal valuable diagnostic information that is worth bringing to the Divine Physician.

℘

A Short Primer on Addiction

The word *addiction* is used in many contexts. Common usage of the term has evolved to include psychological dependence. In this context, the term goes beyond drug addiction and substance abuse problems. It also refers to behaviors that are not generally recognized by the medical community as addictive problems such as compulsive overeating or hoarding.

When the term *addiction* is applied to compulsions that are not substance-related, such as problem gambling and computer addiction, it describes a recurring compulsion one engages in despite the activity's harmful consequences to one's individual physical, mental, social or spiritual health.

Other forms of addiction could be habitual defrauding or tax evasion, money addictions, work addiction, exercise addiction, habitual overeating, habitual shopping, sex addiction, computer addiction, e-mail addiction, video game addiction, pornography addiction, and television addiction.

Gabor Maté sums up addiction's profile: "Addiction is any repeated behavior, substance-related or not, in which a person feels compelled to persist, regardless of its negative impact on his life and the lives of others. Addiction involves:

a. Compulsive engagement with a behavior, or a preoccupation with it.

b. Impaired control over the behavior.

c. Persistence or relapse despite evidence of harm.

d. Dissatisfaction, irritability, or intense craving when the object— be it a drug, activity, or other goal—is not immediately available."[3]

Whew...that was something! Don't get frightened. Remember: *Be Not Afraid: Fear comes from the enemy of my human nature.*

So for this spiritual exercise, do not exceed your twenty-minute prayer period. For this exercise sit apart in a quiet place. Find a comfortable position that permits you to be alert. Breathe deeply for a few minutes, mindful that God's love sustains your very life.

Next, using the personal name for God you identified, ask God to enlighten your memory and imagination so that you can see any addictions you have in the context of your life story.

Before completing your graced remembering, record any addictions that surfaced. Be brief and specific. Identify each addiction by name and frequency: **S**eldom, **O**ften, or **C**onstantly. For example, you may write:

Television—S; Exercise—O; Gambling—C.

An Additional Diagnostic Exercise for Vices and Addictions

If you want to take an additional twenty-minute spiritual exercise today, you can combine this spiritual diagnostic on addictions with the one from day 13 on vices.

Here is how you might do it. You have prayed for the grace to honestly recognize the vices and addictions that erode your freedom and compromise your true self. And you wrote them out in your notebook listing the vices as mild, moderate or strong, and the addictions as seldom, often or constantly.

Begin this spiritual exercise in the standard manner. During your prayer session, review what you wrote in your notebook on vices and addictions, asking Christ, the Divine Physician, in very personal words, to help you discover the *connections* between the vices and addictions.

For example, you may notice that when you are angry, you might move toward one or other addictive behavior. When you are envious, you might be drawn to other addictive behaviors, and so on for the other vices.

Recall that the grace you are asking for is the *inspiration* to *understand* the vices and addictions in and of themselves, and more importantly, to identify the *connections* between them as they manifest in your life story.

When, through grace, you begin to wake up to the links between the thoughts, words and deeds of your life story, then growth in holiness and authenticity can occur.

Before the end the prayer period record any discoveries on links you make between the vices and addictions that God reveals to you. Thank God for the courage to honestly see yourself as you are. Thank God for the grace to wake up to live in greater freedom.

C8

WEEK 2

Optional Meditation

Night Vigil Week 2

This is the second of four night vigils you can do for your Whole-Life Confession journey. We suggest doing them in an evening and giving the meditation 45-minutes.

___TEMPTATION IN THE WILDERNESS___

*Spend forty-five minutes on this meditation. Do only one section at a time and do not read ahead. Do not feel compelled to finish the whole sheet. Stay with each section until your heart suggests moving on. Do not read or write after this meditation except perhaps a short journal entry. **Be Alone.***

I. Gather in what your senses are experiencing. Breathe in the Spirit of God. Breathe out whatever is troubling, distracting, or burdensome. Be aware of all the thoughts and feelings coming from the day so far.

II. Talk to Jesus in your own words about your desire for this particular grace: that I may come to know and believe God the Father as the source of my greatest freedom and that I may come to understand more clearly the source of my greatest imprisonment. Stay with this for as long as you like. Don't feel compelled to move on unless your heart suggests.

III. Imagine yourself accompanying Jesus away from the Jordan River, out into the wilderness. This is the first time each of you has decided to go away, apart from your family and friends. This is your first attempt to spend such a lengthy time in prayer and silence with your God. You are both filled with the Holy Spirit -- yet it is not long before you are faced with the insidious seduction of the spirit of evil and darkness. See and experience the events as they happen. Notice everything about what is happening to Jesus and yourself. Do not move to the next section unless your heart suggests.

Pray with Luke 4: 1-13

IV. ASK THE LORD FOR HIS STRENGTH AND GUIDANCE in facing the temptations, the imprisonments in your life: THE BREAD which represents the material possessions and comforts that you feel you need for status and security; THE POWER of independence, self-sufficiency and pride which keep you, not God, as the center of your life, for not realizing your need for God as the Source of your freedom and life; THE VANITY of self-centeredness which subtly manipulates or exploits others, testing the fidelity of God and others in their love for you. ASK THE LORD FOR HIS HELP in letting go of what binds you; of what keeps you from freely loving others, from freely giving you heart to God, and from freely being your truest self.

V. Following the meditation, bring your own prayer period to a close by slowly praying the *Our Father,* listening to the words in your heart as you pray.

☙

 # Week 3

FIRST

Welcome to week three of your spiritual journey. I will choose a place of contemplative rest and reflection. It will be a place apart—a technology-free zone! I will make a decision where to make my spiritual exercise prayer breaks each day. Regularity is the key to sustainable disciplines of any kind, and is especially true of this prayer relationship with Christ.

SECOND

If there are no specific journal assignments for a given day this week, spend two minutes at the end of the exercise and write a short response to each of these two questions: (by "short" we mean ½ to 2 sentences max—no more!)
1) What in the spiritual exercise today increased my faith, hope and
      love? Be specific and brief.
2) What in the spiritual exercise today decreased my faith, hope and
      love. Be specific but brief.

THIRD

I will ask God for the grace to identify the many links in my Sacred Story between persons, emotions, patterns of sin and grace, virtues and commandments and the important events and experiences of my life. As God enlightens me, I will ask too for the grace to identify the deepest hope of my heart for my life and my future.

Say this litany aloud before each prayer session this week:

I will not read ahead.

I will awaken to the present moment.

I will take each day and each exercise as it comes.

I cannot do Sacred Story better by going faster.

I will ask God to help me.

The Ten Commandments are a profound gift from God
to the Chosen People and to all humankind.

Be Not Afraid:

Fear comes from the enemy of my human nature.

ೞ

Day 15

Read this first:

First, say the litany that begins this week.

Welcome to day fifteen of your spiritual journey. The next three days are powerful exercises on the Decalogue Examination of Conscience. They are to help you better understand your life story and the gift of healing and balance that God desires for you. Pray that your imagination be graced so that the *most important* issues in the Commandments, those that illuminate your history (your <u>story</u>), will come into your mind and heart. Pray to "see" what you have *never* seen before. Pray to see your life as God sees your life.

The Commandments were given to the Chosen People in a Covenant that was sealed with a blood sacrifice. The Church reflects that the power of the animal sacrifice sealing the Covenant receives its power from Christ's blood, which it foreshadows. The Commandments, as *gift,* are a foundation for God's work to repair our broken human nature, to forgive us, and reopen the way to eternity: the work of Christ's death and resurrection. It is no wonder then that laws enshrining the Commandments' truths have transformed stories of violence and injustice to stories of civility and justice for countless millions of people in the last three millennia.

For this exercise, we are reflecting on the Commandments to enhance our understanding of their richness and wisdom. The exercise will help to clarify how each Commandment carries its own responsibilities and boundaries. These *Decrees*—a synonym for *Commandments*— will ignite your imagination so you will be able to hear them differently. These decrees—statements by God—serve as a reminder to us when we have forgotten to *remember and know the truth* about God, humanity and oneself. They are a *gift* to guide our way home so our thoughts, words and deeds bring life, not death.

This may be a helpful format to follow as you reflect on the each Decree. Identify the Decree (and the sub-themes in the Decrees) as mild, moderate, or strong depending on the challenge this specific Decree presents to you. For example, you may write "6th—moderate, especially regarding (issue);" "4th—mild regarding (person);" "7th/10th—strong regarding (event)." Use codes if you prefer to safeguard confidentiality and augment honesty.

The purpose of this exercise is to simply identify your challenges with the Commandments. With Christ by your side, watch with curiosity and detachment, without self-blame. God sees beyond any patterns of sin and failure you have, or think you have. God knows *you* for who you are. God loves you. God is the Divine Physician who desires to help you honestly see your life as it is so He can bring forgiveness, healing, freedom and peace.

Pray that your imagination be graced so that the *most important* issues in the Commandments, those that illuminate your history (your <u>story</u>), will come into your mind and heart. Pray to "see" what you have *never* seen before. Pray to see your life as God sees your life.

Before concluding your prayer period, use your notebook to record where in your life you have missed the mark in living the Decree you reflected on. Be specific, brief, honest and courageous. Ask for the grace of integrity and openness to embrace the truth of your own experience.

THE DECALOGUE EXAMINATION OF CONSCIENCE [4]

First Decree: I am the Lord your God, you shall have no strange gods before me.

Is God the center of my life? Have I displaced God with my career, work, concern for wealth and pleasure? Does the worship and honor of God take shape in my weekly religious practices? Do I pray often? Do I turn to God for forgiveness often? Have I resorted to relying on superstition, the occult or astrology in place of asking for God's assistance?

Second Decree: You shall not take the name of the Lord your God in vain.

Do I casually take God's name in vain? Do I have a habit of swearing in jest or in anger? Do I use God's name to damn other people? Do I nurse hatred of God in my heart? Do I harbor anger towards God for the difficult things in my life or in the world? Do I reverence God in my heart?

Third Decree: Remember to keep holy the Sabbath day.

Do I make every effort to prepare myself for the Sunday Liturgy? Do I make every effort to attend the Sunday Liturgy? Do I allow social or sporting events to displace or limit my attendance at the Sunday Liturgy? Do I limit unnecessary servile work on Sunday? Is Sunday a true day of spiritual rest and refreshment?

Fourth Decree: Honor your Father and Mother.

Do I give proper reverence to my mom and dad for the gift of life? Do I thank them? Do I spend time with them? Do I strive to forgive the shortcomings of my parents? Do I hold anger or grudges against them in my heart? Do I try to respond to them with love and charity? Do I attend to them in their sufferings and weaknesses? Am I patient with their infirmity as they age?

CB

Day 16

Read this first:

First, say the litany that begins this week.

Welcome to day sixteen of your spiritual journey. Remember, the purpose of this exercise is to simply identify your challenges with the Commandments. With Christ by your side, watch with curiosity and detachment, without self-blame. God sees beyond any patterns of sin and failure you have, or think you have. God knows *you* for who you are. God loves you. God is the Divine Physician who desires to help you honestly see your life as it is so He can bring forgiveness, healing, freedom and peace.

Pray that your imagination be graced so that the *most important* issues in the Commandments, those that illuminate your history (your <u>story</u>), will come into your mind and heart. Pray to "see" what you have *never* seen before. Pray to see your life as God sees your life.

Before concluding your prayer period, use your notebook to record where in your life you have missed the mark in living the Decree you reflected on. Be specific, brief, honest and courageous. Ask for the grace of integrity and openness to embrace the truth of your own experience.

THE DECALOGUE EXAMINATION OF CONSCIENCE [5]

Fifth Decree: You shall not kill.

Do I strive to overcome the prejudices I have against individuals or groups? Do I resist acting on my prejudices so as not to harm persons with my words or deeds? Do I act with cruelty towards others? Do I risk my life or the lives of others by using illegal drugs? Do I risk my life or the lives of others by driving recklessly or intoxicated? Do I strive in words and deeds to promote the value of life from conception to natural death? Have I ever helped someone terminate a pregnancy or end his/her own life? Do I strive to do everything I can to uphold the value of each person? Do I harbor satisfaction in my heart at the death of those people whom I consider evil? Do I vote for politicians/civil servants because of their positions to protect and promote abortion, euthanasia, capital punishment or pre-emptive war? Do I mourn the loss of all human life, no matter the cause of death?

Sixth Decree: You shall not commit adultery.

Ninth Decree: You shall not covet your neighbor's spouse.

Do I protect my covenant relationship with my spouse and uphold its sacredness? Do I strive daily to support my spouse? Do I turn to other persons for emotional support to make my spouse envious? Do I denigrate my spouse by comparing her/him to others? Do I speak harshly about my spouse behind his/her back to gain the affections of others? Do I uphold the sacredness of my covenant commitment by never seeking the sexual attention of those to whom I may be attracted? Do I uphold my covenant by never engaging in any sexual activity with someone other than my spouse? Do I use pornography to arouse my sexual appetites, or to avoid intimacy with my spouse? Do I denigrate the spiritual integrity of persons by focusing on their physical beauty or appearance? Do I protect my covenant relationship by not purposely fantasizing about sexual relations with someone other than my spouse? Do I hold sacred the gift of sexuality for marriage? Do I strive to cultivate purity of heart as a sign of God's own single-heartedness? Do I reverence sexual intercourse first and foremost as the gift most akin to God's creative energies, a gift of love to create a human life destined for an eternity with God? Do I casually inhibit God's presence in this divine gift with drugs or medical procedures when there is no legitimate reason?

CB

DAY 17

Read this first:

First, say the litany that begins this week.

Welcome to day seventeen of your spiritual journey. Remember, the purpose of this exercise is to simply identify your challenges with the Commandments. With Christ by your side, watch with curiosity and detachment, without self-blame. God sees beyond any patterns of sin and failure you have, or think you have. God knows *you* for who you are. God loves you. God is the Divine Physician who desires to help you honestly see your life as it is so He can bring forgiveness, healing, freedom and peace.

Pray that your imagination be graced so that the *most important* issues in the Commandments, those that illuminate your history (your <u>story</u>), will come into your mind and heart. Pray to "see" what you have *never* seen before. Pray to see your life as God sees your life.

Before concluding your prayer period, use your notebook to record where in your life you have missed the mark in living the Decree you reflected on. Be specific, brief, honest and courageous. Ask for the grace of integrity and openness to embrace the truth of your own experience.

Seventh Decree: You shall not steal.

Tenth Decree: You shall not covet your neighbor's goods.

Do I cheat on papers and exams to steal a better grade? Do I take things that do not belong to me? Do I keep things I have borrowed? Am I honest in my investments, taxes, and in all my financial dealings? Do I use legal loopholes in tax laws or business practices to harvest financial rewards that ultimately hurt the less fortunate? Am I honest and truthful in my business dealings even if it means I may lose profits or customers? Do I vandalize or harm property or goods that do not belong to me? Do I envy those who have more than I do? Do I let concern for wealth and comfort take center place in my life? Do I live lavishly because I have the resources to do so? Do I spend money on luxury goods I do not need? Do I live with envy of those who have more than I do? Do I respect the limited resources of the earth as a divine inheritance to benefit all people? Do I give a percentage of my earned income to the poor? Do I strive to live so as to minimize waste and protect the environment? Do I examine my investment patterns to discern if companies I own, or in which I have stock, are treating their employees justly and are protecting the environment in their practices? Do I ever put the drive for profits ahead of the welfare of persons or the environment?

Eighth Decree: You shall not bear false witness against your neighbor.

Do I uphold the honor of other people's reputations? Do I avoid spreading gossip and avoid seeking gossip from others? Do I share information about people with third parties, even if it is true, when that information threatens the person's reputation? Do I avoid spreading lies or rumors about other people? Do I challenge people who gossip and spread damaging information about others? Do I avoid and denounce TV, radio, magazines and newspapers that employ the tactics of personality destruction and malicious gossip to sell news and generate profits? Do I tell others what they ought to do instead of getting my own house in order?

CB

Day 18

Read this first:

First, say the litany that begins this week.

Welcome to day eighteen of your spiritual journey. For your exercise today, pray for the grace to remember the books, stories, songs, events, movies and art that have the power to bring you to tears. Pray to remember the turn of phrase, the lyric, the dialogue, the word spoken to you, the melody, and the image that has touched your heart so profoundly that your only response is to weep. The shortest phrase in the Scripture is *"Jesus wept"* (Jn 11: 35). What causes us to weep holds significance in our history, and informs our story. Pray to remember and feel what moves you to tears.

The Gospels record that Jesus wept twice. He wept over Jerusalem, for failing to recognize that the time of its deliverance was at hand (Lk 19: 41-44). And He wept for His good friend Lazarus, "see how he loved him" (Jn 11: 33-6). Both instances reveal Jesus' deep longing for humanity's reconciliation and peace. It is Christ's desire to bring freedom from death's grip, that death which resulted from humanity's disobedience. Jesus' weeping expresses the deepest longings of His heart. His tears reveal His mission in life, a mission He received from the Father, for those He loves.

Tears reveal the deepest longings of our heart. They are a window to the heart and soul. Ask God for the grace to remember and understand what brings you to tears, what breaks your heart or expresses your heart's longings for healing and peace.

Use your 15-minute prayers in the second half of the week to recall what causes you to weep, that is, what brings you to tears and expresses the deepest longings of your heart. Do not spend more than 15-minutes for each of your prayer periods. For your prayer, sit apart in a quiet place. Find a comfortable position that permits you to be alert. Breathe deeply for a few minutes, mindful that God's love sustains your very life.

Next, using the personal name for God you identified, ask God to enlighten your memory and imagination so that you can remember and understand what brings you to tears, and why. Your tears can reveal your heart's truth-your story. What stories, movies, books, songs move you to tears and what can God help you understand about your life from them?

Before your prayer period ends, write down what caused your tears. Record *why* this caused your tears (if it is clear). Reflect further on what this might possibly reveal to you about your story. Do your tears reveal your deepest longings and God's desire to bring you hope and peace?

Cg

Day 19

Read this first:

First, say the litany that begins this week.

Welcome to day nineteen of your spiritual journey. You may give yourself permission to extend this exercise by ten minutes to thirty. The spiritual diagnostic exercise for today offers you the potential for more enlightenment. Spend your time listening to your heart.

Ask God for the grace to discern the key elements in your life story linked to: gratitude; relationships; spiritual, social and financial values; and those you need to forgive, or whose forgiveness you need accept.

Take a few minutes for each of the six spiritual diagnostics. Deciphering these can help you see the two plot-lines in your life history more clearly. Be sure to ask for God's assistance and use the personal name for God to ask for the grace for each goal revel the most important insights for your life story.

For your journal exercise, write one short phrase at the end of each goal: one phrase capturing an aspect of what you wrote that increases your faith, hope and love, and one aspect that diminished the same. The short phrase does not even need to be a full sentence. Be specific but brief!

GRATITUDE GOAL

I ask God for the grace to remember the one experience, event or person for which I am most grateful. It could be a kindness someone showed me. It could be a loving gesture from a parent, friend, husband, wife or child. It could be something that did *not* happen to me—some danger or threat, sickness or accident that was avoided or minimized. It could be some significant event in my life that moved me in a new direction. It could be a spiritual experience that opened me to a deeper hope and joy in my life. What comes to mind? I will pray for the grace to recall the feelings I felt at the time of the event and take note of the reasons why. I pray to see connections in my responses to other prayer exercises as they occur. Before I finish my prayer, I will write my memory in one sentence below and why it inspires gratitude.

Example: My brother with Down's syndrome brought our family together and made us realize the true meaning of life and love.

RELATIONAL GOAL

I ask God for the grace to identify the most important relational goal I can imagine for my life story. It could be with God, my spouse, my children, my family or a close friend. This is the one relational goal that if I accomplished it, would cause me to believe my life was fulfilled. I will look for connections in my responses to other prayer exercises as they occur to me. Before I finish my prayer, I will write my relationship goal in one sentence below and why it would define my relational success.

Example: That I can be a faithful father and husband for life.

SPIRITUAL GOAL

I ask God for the grace to understand my most hoped for spiritual goal for my life story. It could be with God, my spouse, my children, my family or a close friend. It is the one spiritual goal that if I accomplished it, would cause me to believe that my life was fulfilled. I will look for connections in my responses to other prayer exercises as they occur to me. Before I finish my prayer, I will write my spiritual goal in one sentence below and why it would define spiritual success for me.

Example: That I do something every day to strengthen my relationship with God and also one thing to serve those most in need.

SOCIETAL GOAL

I ask God for the grace to understand my most hoped for societal or political goal for my life story. It could be with God, or for my spouse, my children, my family, a close friend or for the Church, the country or the world. It is the one societal goal that if I accomplished it, or helped accomplish it, would cause me to believe my life was fulfilled. I will look for connections in my responses to other prayer exercises as they occur to me. Before I finish my prayer, I will write my societal goal in one sentence below and why it would define social success for me and the world.

Example: That I will not be afraid to take a stand to help promote a culture that respects life from conception till death.

FINANCIAL GOAL

I will ask God the grace to understand my most hoped for financial or economic goal or ambition for my life story. It could be for God, my spouse, my children, my family, a close friend or for the Church, country or the world. It is the one financial goal that if I accomplished it, or helped accomplish it, would cause me to believe my life was fulfilled. I will look for connections in my responses to other prayer exercises as they occur to me. Before I finish my prayer, I will write my financial goal in one sentence below and why it would define financial success for me.

Example: That I work to live and not live to work and that I can teach my children that living simply is the source of joy.

FORGIVENESS GOAL

I ask God for the grace to understand the one person who would be most grateful to receive my forgiveness. I also ask God for the grace to understand the one person whose forgiveness I would be most grateful to receive. Before finishing my prayer, I will write two short sentences below, one for each person, describing why gratitude would be present in each instance of forgiveness.

Example: That I will continue to ask God to help me forgive my parents for getting divorced and breaking our family apart.

ෆ

Day 20

Read this first:

First, say the litany that begins this week.

Welcome to day twenty of your spiritual journey. As usual I will pray with personal words from my heart to see what I have not seen before, **and** to see connections between aspects of my life story. I am invited to watch these components of my life narrative with the Divine Physician by my side. Christ invites me to *wake up* in my life.

You are only in the beginning period of attempting, with God's grace, to see your history more clearly. Your goal is to better understand how to listen to your *history, both its challenges and its hopes.* Remember, Christ watches with you with love, patience, compassion and infinite mercy. BE NOT AFRAID!

For your spiritual exercise today, go back over your journal notes and ask to be inspired to see what God wants you to see at this time. Use the person name for God and say: "Give the eyes and heart to see what will help me most at this time in my life." Now, look at what jotted down in your journal for these days:

Eleven: Gratitude, Hope, Love

Twelve: Fear, Anger, Grief

Thirteen: Vices

Fourteen: Addictions

Fifteen-Seventeen: Decalogue Commandments

Eighteen: Things that bring me to tears

Nineteen: Goals

When you finish reading your reflections, write two simple sentences in your journal that answer these questions: One- What gave me the greatest sense of faith, hope and love? Two-What gave me the greatest reason to doubt faith, hope and love. Two single sentences, no more.

CB

Day 21

Read this first:

First, say the litany that begins this week.

Welcome to day twenty-one of your spiritual journey. As usual I will pray with personal words from my heart to see what I have not seen before, **and** to see connections between aspects of my life story. I am invited to watch these components of my life narrative with the Divine Physician by my side. Christ invites me to *wake up* in my life.

You are only in the beginning period of attempting, with God's grace, to see your history more clearly. Your goal is to better understand how to listen to your history, both its challenges and its hopes. Remember, Christ watches with you with love, patience, compassion and infinite mercy. BE NOT AFRAID!

For your spiritual exercise today, fill in the diagnostic chart (Looking for Links in My Story) *with at least one element* for each of the statements provided.

LOOKING FOR LINKS IN MY STORY

A COMMANDMENT THAT CHALLENGES ME	
VICES THAT ENSNARE ME	

ADDICTIONS I LIVE WITH	
PERSONS/EVENTS THAT GENERATE FEAR, ANGER OR GRIEF	
PERSONS/EVENTS THAT GENERATE FAITH, HOPE OR LOVE	
STORY LINES IN BOOKS, MOVIES. THAT ALWAYS BRING ME TO TEARS	
WHAT ALWAYS MAKES ME ANGRY	
WHAT ALWAYS MAKES ME GRATEFUL	
WHAT ALWAYS INSPIRES FEAR IN ME	
MY ULTIMATE FAITH GOAL	
THE AREA OF MY LIFE MOST OUT OF CONTROL	

When you finish reading your reflections, write two simple sentences in your journal that answer these questions: One- What gave me the greatest sense of faith, hope and love? Two-What gave me the greatest reason to doubt faith, hope and love. Two single sentences, no more.

ℭℨ

WEEK 3

Optional Meditation

Night Vigil Week 3 [6]

This is the third of four night vigils you can do for your Whole-Life Confession journey. We suggest doing them in an evening and giving the meditation 45-minutes.

<u>DO NOT BE AFRAID!</u>

Be open to all thoughts, feelings, and ideas you have coming from the day. Spend some time talking with God about the things you think significant. Stay here as long as you are comfortable. Be Alone.

I. Begin this meditation by asking Jesus to be with you. Ask Jesus to give you the graces he feels will be best for you during this time of the night vigil and this time of training. Specifically ask for the grace to know the good you desire and how you can be tempted to believe that Jesus is not working in your or love you when you feel your weakness and sinfulness. Pray for the grace to know why you can feel bad when God is actually energizing your conscience to know your True Heart. Use the *Triple Colloquy* below to ask for these graces.

II. Open your Bible to the fifth chapter of Luke, verses one to eleven. Before you read, plan to read it slowly so you can visualize the scenes as they really happened; only place yourself on the boat as one of the disciples. Notice all the details of the people, the smells, the sounds, etc. Keep aware of all the thoughts and feelings you had entering this meditation; only now let yourself be distracted by the events as they unfold before you.

* What is Peter's dilemma? Can you sense what he may be feeling as he speaks to Jesus and asks him to leave him? What is Jesus' response? What does Jesus offer him? Speak to Peter after he is invited by Jesus to be a fisher of people. What is his joy or confusion? What does he say?

III. Pay attention to your reaction to the events that have unfolded before you. See the man leave the presence of Jesus. Walk up to Jesus from your place in the crowd. You are present before Jesus so no one else in the crowd can hear you. Speak to Jesus about what you have just seen and heard. What do you say? What does he say?

IV. Ask Jesus if there is anything in your own life that would prevent you from being a disciple of his. Ask Jesus about any particular things in your own life that cause you shame and make you think Jesus could not or does not love you. What do you say? What is Jesus' response? Stop and listen. What are you thinking and feeling?

V. Pray: *Take, Lord, and receive all my liberty, my memory, my understanding, and my entire will; all that I have and possess. You have given all to me. To you, Lord, I return it. Everything is yours; dispose of it according to your will. Give me only your love and your grace. That is enough for me. Amen!*

TRIPLE COLLOQUY OF SAINT IGNATIUS

First Colloquy, or conversation, will be with Mary. Speak with Mary, using your own words asking her to obtain from her Son the grace to follow her Son in every act and decision of your life. When you finish this conversation, pray the *Hail Mary* slowly, thinking of the words and the person to whom you are praying.

Hail Mary, full of grace, The Lord is with thee.
Blessed art thou amongst women
and blessed is the fruit of thy womb, Jesus.
Holy Mary, Mother of God, Pray for us sinners,
now and at the hour of our death.
Amen.

Second Colloquy, or conversation, will be with Jesus. Speak directly to Jesus, asking him to request his Father for the same graces as above, i.e., that you may follow Jesus. When you finish your conversation, pray the *Anima Christi* slowly, thinking of the words and the person to whom you are praying.

Soul of Christ, sanctify me. Body of Christ, save me.
Blood of Christ, inebriate me. Water from the side of Christ wash me.
Passion of Christ, strengthen me. O Good Jesus, hear me.
Within thy wounds, hide me. Permit me not to be separated from thee.
From the wicked foe, defend me. At the hour of my death, call me,
And bid me come to thee that with thy saints I may praise thee forever
and ever.
Amen.

Third Colloquy, or conversation, will be with God the Father. Ask the Father directly in your own words to give you the graces so you may follow His Son. When you finish, pray the *Our Father*, thinking of the words and the person to whom you are praying.

Our Father, Who art in heaven, hallowed be thy name. Thy Kingdom come, Thy will be done, on earth as it is in heaven.
Give us this day our daily bread, and forgive us our trespasses,
As we forgive those who trespass against us.
Lead us not into temptation, but deliver us from evil. Amen.

CG

Week 4

FIRST

Welcome to week four of your spiritual journey. I will choose a place of contemplative rest and reflection. It will be a place apart—a technology-free zone! I will make a decision where to make my spiritual exercise prayer breaks each day. Regularity is the key to sustainable disciplines of any kind, and is especially true of this prayer relationship with Christ.

SECOND

If there are no specific journal assignments for a given day this week, spend two minutes at the end of the exercise and write a short response to each of these two questions: (by "short" we mean ½ to 2 sentences max—no more!)
1) What in the spiritual exercise today increased my faith, hope and love? Be specific and brief.
2) What in the spiritual exercise today decreased my faith, hope and love. Be specific but brief.

THIRD

I will *ask for the grace to see connections between aspects of my life story.* I am invited to watch these components of my life narrative with the Divine Physician by my side. Christ invites me not to be afraid but to *wake up* in my life—my *spiritual* life. I will watch and pray with Christ. My spiritual exercises for this fourth week consist of exercises that are preparing me to write my Whole-Life Confession. I will use the personal name for God I have discovered and I will invoke that holy name in all of my times of prayer and whenever it comes to me in the middle of the day.

THE WHOLE-LIFE CONFESSION

Say this litany aloud before each prayer session this week:

I will not read ahead.

I will awaken to the present moment.

I will take each day and each exercise as it comes.

I cannot do better by going faster.

I will ask God to help me.

Fear comes from the enemy of my human nature.

I affirm that everything that has happened to me, and everything I have experienced in my entire life, is present in my memory.

Lord Jesus Christ, I affirm you will always transform my sin and weakness into grace and blessings!

I will not be afraid!

☞

Day 22

Read this first:

I will say this affirmation aloud today as often as I remember to:

Lord Jesus Christ, I affirm you will always transform my sin and weakness into grace and blessings! I will not be afraid!

Welcome to day twenty-two of your spiritual journey. As usual I will pray with personal words from my heart to see what I have not seen before, *and* to see connections between aspects of my life story. I am invited to watch these components of my life narrative with the Divine Physician by my side. Christ invites me to *wake up* in my life.

You are only in the beginning period of attempting, with God's grace, to see your history more clearly. Your goal is to better understand how to listen to your history, both its challenges and its hopes. Remember, Christ watches with you with love, patience, compassion and infinite mercy. BE NOT AFRAID!

For your spiritual exercise today, fill in the diagnostic chart (Looking for Links in My Story) *with at least one element* for each of the statements provided.

When you finish your chart, write two simple sentences in your journal that answer these questions: One- What gave me the greatest sense of faith, hope and love? Two-What gave me the greatest reason to doubt faith, hope and love. Two single sentences, no more.

Important Note: The data from your life diagnostic charts will be helpful to you throughout your life. You are only in the beginning period of attempting, with God's grace, to see your history of grace and sin more clearly. Your goal is to better understand how to listen to your *Sacred*

Story. Remember, Christ watches with you with love, patience, compassion and infinite mercy your whole-life long. Be Not Afraid!

ɞ

LOOKING FOR LINKS IN MY STORY

I fill in the second diagnostic chart below with the goal to write at least 3 things requested in each category.

THREE COMMANDMENTS I AM MOST CHALLENGED IN LIVING	THREE VICES THAT ENSNARE ME	THREE ADDICTIONS I LIVE WITH	THREE PERSONS/EVENTS THAT CAUSE FEAR, ANGER OR GRIEF

THREE COMMANDMENTS I AM MOST CHALLENGED IN LIVING	THREE VICES THAT ENSNARE ME	THREE ADDICTIONS I LIVE WITH	THREE PERSONS/EVENTS THAT CAUSE FEAR, ANGER OR GRIEF

ଔ

Day 23

Read this first:

I will say this affirmation aloud today as often as I remember to:

Lord Jesus Christ, I affirm you will always transform my sin and weakness into grace and blessings! I will not be afraid!

Welcome to day twenty-three of your spiritual journey. As usual I will pray with personal words from my heart to see what I have not seen before, *and* to see connections between aspects of my life story. I am invited to watch these components of my life narrative with the Divine Physician by my side. Christ invites me to *wake up* in my life.

You are only in the beginning period of attempting, with God's grace, to see your history more clearly. Your goal is to better understand how to listen to your history, both its challenges and its hopes. Remember, Christ watches with you with love, patience, compassion and infinite mercy. BE NOT AFRAID!

For my spiritual exercise today, I will contemplate the next diagnostic chart of how sin impacted the life of St. Ignatius to see the links in his original (root), core (trunk), and manifest (fruit) sins.

When you finish your chart, write two simple sentences in your journal that answer these questions: One- What gave me the greatest sense of faith, hope and love? Two-What gave me the greatest reason to doubt faith, hope and love. Two single sentences, no more.

೮౧

MANIFEST SINS
The Fruit or Ornamentation
(Ignatius' addictive gambling, reactive anger and sexual self-indulgence)
*Manifest Fear, Anger, and Grief, moral weaknesses, vices,
addictions, and sinful habits that are the
most visible to you.*

CORE SINS
The Trunk or Superstructure
(Ignatius' arrogance, blinded conscience and narcissism)
*Disobedience and narcissism, along with its fear, anger, and grief,
that forms the trunk or superstructure of your daily life, feeding on
originating sins and events.*

ORIGINAL SINS
The Roots or Foundation
(Original Sin and concupiscence that wounded Ignatius' heart and
soul; distinctive family/clan sin and/or early life-events that
wounded him spiritually,
psychologically and physically)
*Ancient, originating events that rooted the patterns of disobedience
and narcissism along
with its Fear, Anger, Grief.*

℘

Day 24

Read this first:

I will say this affirmation aloud today as often as I remember to:

Lord Jesus Christ, I affirm you will always transform my sin and weakness into grace and blessings! I will not be afraid!

Welcome to day twenty-four of your spiritual journey. As usual I will pray with personal words from my heart to see what I have not seen before, **and** to see connections between aspects of my life story. I am invited to watch these components of my life narrative with the Divine Physician by my side. Christ invites me to *wake up* in my life.

You are only in the beginning period of attempting, with God's grace, to see your history more clearly. Your goal is to better understand how to listen to your history, both its challenges and its hopes. Remember, Christ watches with you with love, patience, compassion and infinite mercy. BE NOT AFRAID!

For my spiritual exercise today, I contemplate the elements from the diagnostic charts I filled in earlier in the week and I pray for the grace to see more clearly how sin has impacted me at the roots, trunk and fruit of my life. For each of the blank spaces on the last chart, I will write those elements (at least one each) that I believe are present in my life as Original Sins (root), core sins (trunk) and manifest sins (fruit).

When you finish reading your reflections, write two simple sentences in your journal that answer these questions: One- What gave me the greatest sense of faith, hope and love? Two-What gave me the greatest reason to doubt faith, hope and love. Two single sentences, no more.

LOOKING FOR LINKS IN MY STORY

MY MANIFEST SINS—THE FRUIT FROM MY TREE

↓   ↑

MY CORE SINS—THE TRUNK OF MY TREE

↓   ↑

MY ORIGINAL SINS—THE ROOTS OF MY TREE

Day 25

Read this first:

I will say this affirmation aloud today as often as I remember to:

Lord Jesus Christ, I affirm you will always transform my sin and weakness into grace and blessings! I will not be afraid!

Welcome to day twenty-five of your spiritual journey. As usual I will pray with personal words from my heart to see what I have not seen before, **and** to see connections between aspects of my life story. I am invited to watch these components of my life narrative with the Divine Physician by my side. Christ invites me to *wake up* in my life. For my spiritual exercise today, I will simply read about the Whole-Life Confession.

When you finish reading about the Whole-Life Confession, write two simple sentences in your journal that answer these questions: One-What gave me the greatest sense of faith, hope and love? Two-What gave me the greatest reason to doubt faith, hope and love. Two single sentences, no more.

A LETTER TO CHRIST JESUS

You may be wondering how you will make use of the prayer exercises from the past few weeks. This will become clearer as your journey continues. Have faith that your efforts will be spiritually fruitful. You are not expected to see the complete picture in everything you have done so far.

We have been on a treasure hunt of sorts, pulling together many diverse elements of our life story. The process of piecing the parts together will happen throughout the rest of your life—both by your careful attention and by the grace of God. So, have patience and trust.

As time goes on, everything you have done up to this point will take on greater meaning for you (if you follow the lessons in order *and* ask for God's help).

For the following day's spiritual exercises, you will prepare your Whole-Life Confession. Your journal notes from the previous weeks should be very valuable in this sacred process.

What do we mean by a Whole-Life Confession? A Whole-Life Confession is different from a confession of your whole life. It is not helpful, nor is it required to twice confess sins and faults you have already confessed. The opportunity of a Whole-Life Confession is to look at connections and patterns of sin and failure across *your whole life*—what we have been working on these past weeks. You are invited to ask for God's help to see a holistic picture of your life—your story—with Christ as your Divine Physician and healer.

It must be recalled that this reconciliation with God leads, as it were, to other reconciliations, which repair the other breaches caused by sin. The forgiven penitent is reconciled with himself in his inmost being, where he regains his innermost truth. He is reconciled with his brethren whom he has in some way offended and wounded. He is reconciled with the Church. He is reconciled with all creation.[7]

Think of this confession as your report to Christ—based on your spiritual diagnosis—after these weeks of prayerful reflection. You can confess current issues and past issues that have been overlooked. As you do this, you are telling Christ the chronic *patterns* of sin and weaknesses your prayer and reflection with the help of God's grace has awakened in you. And, importantly, how these issues are *linked* to your life story—your history.

Look at your life story with Christ the Divine Physician by your side. Address Him directly and acknowledge why you need Him as your Savior. This *could* be the very first time you have reviewed your life, seen clearly why you cannot save yourself, and directly asked Jesus to be your Savior. What a profound grace to know why you cannot save yourself and to ask Christ for this tremendous gift! A profound grace, indeed!

Look at this from Christ's perspective, too. There is no greater gift you give to Christ than your sinfulness and weaknesses as you ask for His healing love, mercy and forgiveness. By doing so, you take seriously the gift of His life, passion, death and resurrection. You are telling Jesus you need His cross to be healed. You are thanking Jesus for suffering and dying for *you* so you can be renewed in Him. This is the real focus of Christian life! Jesus really loves you and wants to hear what you have to say to Him. He waits with compassion and great longing to hear your story. He waits to carry your burdens and to offer you His forgiveness.

The Pharisees and their scribes complained to his disciples, saying, "Why do you eat and drink with tax collectors and sinners?" Jesus said to them in reply, "Those who are healthy do not need a physician, but the sick do. I have not come to call the righteous to repentance but sinners." Lk 5: 30-32

With Jesus as your Divine Physician, a Whole-Life Confession makes *perfect* sense. He understands you and everything about your life. He has an intense desire to hear your life story and wants to respond as your Savior. What follows are a few suggestions to help you prepare for this simple, holy and graced letter. Your letter is a statement of your need and a confession of your sins and patterns of sin, as well as a request for forgiveness, healing and hope:

1. One picture is worth a thousand words —

Your life is a picture, a story. Write a letter to Christ that is *no more* than 1000 words. If typed, it would be about three and a half pages double-spaced. But you do not have to write that much. I repeat: write *no more* than 1000 words.

Personal words that are heartfelt—

ly on you identified the name for God that touches your heart. This
ek find the name for Christ that speaks to your heart. Perhaps it is
rist Jesus, Lord and Savior or My Lord. You are speaking to the One
ho won your victory and who came into the world to save you. This
eek, we want to speak directly to Christ Jesus. Speak to Jesus in the
first person: "Please forgive…; I remember; I suffered; please heal
me…." Write the confessional story—your history—directly from your
heart to the heart of Jesus.

3. Strive for honesty—

Strive earnestly for courage and honesty in your letter. The letter is for
you and you only, unless you choose to share it in Sacramental
Confession. You need not impress anyone. What is significant is your
courage and honesty. Be honest too, about the forgiveness you need to
extend to others. *Write from your heart.*

4. You are not climbing Mount Everest—

PLEASE, pray for the grace not to turn this simple, graced
letter/confession opportunity into a huge, exhausting task. You are not
climbing a mountain. You are having a conversation with Christ about
your life. Hear Him say to you:

*Come to me, all you who labor and are burdened, and I will give you
rest. Take my yoke upon you and learn from me, for I am meek and
humble of heart; and you will find rest for your selves. For my yoke is
easy and my burden light.* Mt 11: 28-29

5. Pray for Patience and Compassion—

Awakening to your life story will take the rest of your life. It takes a
lifetime for Christ's work of healing and forgiveness to embrace your
heart and soul. There is no finish line or ultimate enlightenment you can
reach on this earth. You will always need healing at deeper levels. You

will constantly grow in love and enlightenment, selflessness and humility until the day you pass from this earth. You will not be finished until the day the Divine Physician sits you down at His Eternal Banquet.

But as for the seed that fell on rich soil, they are the ones who, when they have heard the word, embrace it with a generous and good heart, and bear fruit through perseverance. Lk 8:15

6. Set the scene in your heart's imagination—

Here is how you might set your heart's imagination as you write: imagine you have been given the opportunity to be alone with Christ when He is walking from one town to another. You will have 15-minutes with Him...alone. See the road and the other followers walking up ahead of you and the Lord. No one else can hear you. Write your letter as if you are speaking to Christ in this setting. He knows why you want to speak with Him and is ready to hear you. Before you begin talking about your life, He looks you in the eyes and says: "Soon, I will be lifted up on my cross. I am doing this for you so that you can find forgiveness, healing and hope for the sins, weaknesses and suffering you experience in your life. As I conquer all death and sin—as I breathe my last breath— I will hold you and your life story in my heart. You will find victory and eternal life in me and one day you will be with me in paradise."

Then Jesus said, "Father, forgive them, they know not what they do." Then he said, "Jesus, remember me when you come into your kingdom." He replied to him, "Amen, I say to you, today you will be with me in Paradise." Lk 23: 34, 42-3.

Sample Letter to Jesus

What follows is a template for how you might structure your heart-felt conversation/letter/confession to Christ Jesus, the Divine Physician:

✠   "Dear Jesus, I am so grateful for all the gifts you have given to me." (Spend some time writing from your heart why you are grateful. Use the name of Jesus often as you write your letter, giving *very particular* examples of why you are grateful).

✠ "Lord, I am profoundly aware of how some of my past experiences (life history, family, friends, work, school, neighbors) are linked to areas of un-freedom in my life and how these experiences have created embarrassing and/or discouraging habits and rooted patterns of sinfulness." (Spend some time looking back over your life and offer particular examples that capture the links and patterns of sins, addictions, vices, and commandments that cause you to stumble. If you cannot discern patterns yet, simply speak about these areas individually. If there are central people in your life story who are linked to these destructive patterns, mention them to Christ. If you are confused about some of the things you do, tell Jesus what they are and then, ask for His help to better understand why you do what you do. From your heart, ask Christ's grace to gain greater freedom from these sins and patterns of sin, habits and vices).

✠ "But Lord, there is one central pattern of sin that causes me the most embarrassment, shame, confusion and discouragement." (Spend some time being very specific in your conversation with Jesus about this pattern of sin in your life and why it is so difficult for you. Tell Jesus the particular circumstances when you seem to fall under its spell the most and the circumstances that surround your failures. Tell Jesus how you feel when you fail. If there are specific incidents of this pattern of failure that you have not confessed, tell them to the Lord, and ask for His healing and forgiveness).

✠ "Lord Jesus, I have come to realize that I cannot save myself and I ask for your compassion. I ask that you be my Savior. Rescue me and be with me all the rest of my days." (Spend some time speaking with Jesus, in very particular words, about why you have come to realize you cannot save yourself and why you need His grace—why you need Him to be your Savior. Tell Him in very clear words why you know—because of x, y and z—why you cannot save yourself. Tell Him about any persons you cannot forgive and what they did to you. Tell Him why it is difficult for you to forgive them. Tell Jesus that with His grace, you can desire to forgive them, and in time, be able to forgive them. Ask for that grace. Ask the Lord to keep His attention on the core issues in your life (name them) that constantly trip you up, and pray that you never tire in seeking His forgiveness and that you never lose hope in yourself or in Him. Ask the Lord to be your Savior).

✠ "Lord Jesus, I thank you that you have given me the courage to face any fears I had and to trust you with my life in this healing sacrament of your redeeming love." (Close your letter/conversation/confession with very personal words from your heart, thanking Jesus that He has heard your prayer and that He will always be your Savior. With heartfelt words, thank Jesus that He understands your life and ask that He continue to walk with you, give you grace, and be with you till the end of your days. Ask Jesus for the grace to serve Him more each day with everything you think, say and do. Ask for the grace to work for fruit that will endure to eternity).

✠ "Thank you Jesus for being my Savior." (Close your heartfelt letter by thanking Jesus for being your Savior. Ask for His continued grace as He writes your *Sacred Story*).

☙

Day 26

Read this first:

I will say this affirmation aloud today as often as I remember to:

Lord Jesus Christ, I affirm you will always transform my sin and weakness into grace and blessings! I will not be afraid!

Welcome to day twenty-six of your spiritual journey. As usual I will pray with personal words from my heart to see what I have not seen before, **and** to see connections between aspects of my life story. I am invited to watch these components of my life narrative with the Divine Physician by my side. Christ invites me to *wake up* in my life.

My spiritual exercise today and tomorrow is to write a letter to Christ Jesus asking for His help and healing for my life story. The letter is my confession of faith in Him who comes to heal me and forgive me. The letter is also a snapshot of my whole life. It is my opportunity to tell Christ where I have been wounded by sin, life's difficulties, how I struggle for wholeness and why I need Jesus' help and forgiveness. I will ask Jesus to be my Savior.

My spiritual exercise today and tomorrow can be longer than 20-minutes, because I am writing a letter. Nevertheless, I still begin each prayer period by sitting in a comfortable position. I will use my favorite name for Jesus (Christ Jesus, Lord and Savior, Redeemer…), for this week's personal prayer because Christ is the person who won my freedom from sin and death. This week, He is the one to whom I am speaking.

Remember the guidelines for this letter from Day 25

Remember all the guidelines from Day 25 for this letter. Your letter to Christ is to be *no more* than 1000 words. If typed, it would be about three and a half pages double-spaced. But you do not have to write that much. I repeat: write *no more* than 1000 words. Also use the template for the Sample Letter to Jesus from Day 25 for your own letter.

ℭ♌

Day 27

Read this first:

I will say this affirmation aloud today as often as I remember to:

Lord Jesus Christ, I affirm you will always transform my sin and weakness into grace and blessings! I will not be afraid!

Welcome to day twenty-seven of your spiritual journey. As usual I will pray with personal words from my heart to see what I have not seen before, **and** to see connections between aspects of my life story. I am invited to watch these components of my life narrative with the Divine Physician by my side. Christ invites me to *wake up* in my life.

My spiritual exercise today is to finish writing a letter to Christ Jesus asking for His help and healing for my life story. The letter is my confession of faith in Him who comes to heal me and forgive me. The letter is also a snapshot of my whole life. It is my opportunity to tell Christ where I have been wounded by sin, life's difficulties, how I struggle for wholeness and why I need Jesus' help and forgiveness. I will ask Jesus to be my Savior.

My spiritual exercise today can be longer than 20-minutes, because I am writing a letter. Nevertheless, I still begin each prayer period by sitting in a comfortable position. I will use my favorite name for Jesus (Christ Jesus, Lord and Savior, Redeemer...), for this week's personal prayer because Christ is the person who won my freedom from sin and death. This week, He is the one to whom I am speaking.

Remember the guidelines for this letter from Day 25

☙

Day 28

Read this first:

I will say this affirmation aloud today as often as I remember to:

Lord Jesus Christ, I affirm you will always transform my sin and weakness into grace and blessings! I will not be afraid!

Welcome to day twenty-eight of your spiritual journey. As usual I will pray with personal words from my heart to see what I have not seen before, **and** to see connections between aspects of my life story. I am invited to watch these components of my life narrative with the Divine Physician by my side. Christ invites me to *wake up* in my life.

We are a people of faith who live in the light of the Cross of Christ, the light of the Resurrection of Christ and the light of the Second Coming of Christ. We are His sisters and brothers. We live because we are loved by God.

During these days as you reflect on your Whole-Life Confession, remember that confession includes grateful praise along with admission of sins and faults. Remember that Christ, the Divine Physician, came so that you can triumph *through* your failings and weaknesses, by His healing and forgiving grace, to produce fruit that endures to eternity.

Remember how St. Ignatius marveled once that he did not think, in the entire history of the Church, there was ever someone who sinned as much as he did, who was also given so many graces. "Where sin increased, grace overflowed all the more." (Rom 5:20).

Today is your time to take your Whole-Life Confession letter to Reconciliation. Do not surrender to your anxiety or perfectionism that may suggest that you have not written a "perfect" letter.

If you have made your confession, use your 20-minute prayer period today to be with Christ and the letter you wrote to Him. Bring your notebook to your prayer sessions.

After each session, write one sentence for what brings you the most hope as you read your letter, and one sentence for what causes you the most discouragement as you read your letter. Linger over the words and phrases that brought you hope and peace. Remember the experience of your confession and allow its graces to penetrate deeply into your heart.

CB

WEEK 4

Optional Meditation

Night Vigil Week 4 [8]

This is the fourth of four night vigils you can do for your Whole-Life Confession journey. We suggest doing them in an evening and giving the meditation 45-minutes.

RESURRECTION OF LAZARUS

Do only one section at a time. Move ahead as your heart suggests. Spend as long as you like on the last section. **Be Alone.**

I. Pray to Jesus, begging for the grace of the knowledge of those areas of your life where sin's darkness and confusion are the most shaming and damaging. This is a graced insight that can only be given to us by the Lord. We are incapable of knowing our sinfulness apart from his love showing us the way. Pray to Jesus, using your own words.

II. Open your Bible to the Eleventh Chapter of John and read verses one through forty-four. It is a familiar story but try to read it anew, paying attention to all the details; the people, locations, sights, and smells. See the reactions of the various people -- notice their moods, hopes, fears, etc. Spend as much time as you like doing this and move ahead when your heart suggests.

III. Read the same passage again through verse thirty-seven but this time read the story substituting your name and hometown in place of Lazarus and Bethany. Read slowly and pay attention to your own thoughts and feelings as you do. What do you notice, feel and comprehend?

IV. Read the remaining part of the story, verses thirty-eight through forty-four. Understand that Jesus has come to give you healing and new life -- that he has come to call out of the tomb. As he weeps, understand it is because of his love for you he does so. See yourself in the tomb. What parts of your life need to be brought back to life – where is forgiveness and healing most needed? Ask Jesus to raise you to life. Hear Jesus calling you from the tomb -- as he does so, hear him name all those areas of your life you have just named where you need hope and forgiveness. Hear his words of forgiveness and compassion as he calls you forth and embraces you. Stop. What are you thinking and feeling? Listen.

V. End your time of meditation slowly praying the words of the *Our Father.*

CB

SACRED STORY PRAYER MEDITATIONS

Pray the whole 15-minute Sacred Story *prayer below once or twice daily and consciously repeat to Christ Jesus the five-word refrain (Creation, Presence, Memory, Mercy & Eternity) whenever you are in the grip of fear, anxiety, grief or sins, addictions and destructive compulsions.*

CREATION

I believe God created everything in love and for love; I ask for heart-felt knowledge of God's love for me, and for gratitude for the general and particular graces of this day.

PRESENCE

I believe God is present in each moment and event of my life, and I ask for the grace to awaken, see and feel where and how, especially in this present moment.

MEMORY

I believe every violation of love committed by me and against me is in my memory, and I ask God to reveal them to me, especially those that have manifested themselves today, so I can be healed.

MERCY

I believe that forgiveness is the only path to healing and illumination. I beg for the grace of forgiveness, and the grace to forgive, especially for the general and particular failures of this day, and from my past.

ETERNITY

I believe the grace of forgiveness opens my heart, making my every thought, word and deed bear fruit that endures to eternity. I ask that everything in my life serve Christ's Great Work of Reconciliation.

ജ

Take Lord, receive, my liberty, my memory, my understanding, my entire will. Whatsoever I have or hold, You have given to me. I surrender it all back to you to be governed by your will. Give me only Your love and grace. This is enough for me, and I ask for nothing more. Amen.

ജ

Your ways, O Lord, make known to me; teach me your paths.
Guide me in your truth and teach me, for you are God my savior,
and for you I wait all the day.
Good and upright is the Lord; thus he shows sinners the way.
He guides the humble to justice, and teaches the humble his way.
All the paths of the Lord are kindness and constancy
toward those who keep his covenant and his decrees.
The friendship of the Lord is with those who fear him,
and his covenant, for their instruction.
(Ps 25: 4-5, 8-9, 10, 14)

ഇ

Abide in Me

A Daily Relationship with Christ as Savior,

Divine Physician and Lord of All [9]

I invite you to pray with the first few verses of chapter fifteen from the Gospel of St. John. Take as many minutes, hours or days as you wish to pray with St. John. There is no hurry.

I am the true vine, and my Father is the vinedresser. Every branch of mine that bears no fruit, he takes away, and every branch that does bear fruit he prunes, that it may bear more fruit. You are already made clean by the word which I have spoken to you. Abide in me, and I in you. As the branch cannot bear fruit by itself, unless it abides in the vine, neither can you, unless you abide in me. I am the vine, you are the branches. He who abides in me, and I in him, he it is that bears much fruit, for apart from me you can do nothing. If a man does not abide in me, he is cast forth as a branch and withers; and the branches are gathered, thrown into the fire and burned. If you abide in me, and my words abide in you, ask whatever you will, and it shall be done for you. By this my Father is glorified, that you bear much fruit, and so prove to be my disciples. As the Father has loved me, so have I loved you; abide in my love. If you keep my commandments, you will abide in my love, just as I have kept my Father's commandments and abide in his love. These things I have spoken to you, that my joy may be in you, and that your joy may be full. (Jn 15: 4-11)

The Ignatian *Examen* that inspires *Sacred Story* prayer became an active part of my Jesuit life in 1994. Having entered the Society of Jesus in 1973, I had already lived for twenty years as a Jesuit—eight of those years as a priest. My practice of this prayer was inconstant for many years. By most measures, one could say that I *had* a Christian vocation. I mean this in much the same way that one looking at a Catholic married couple with children or a single person doing service work would say that each of these persons *have* a Christian vocation.

A life of prayer and daily Mass, a yearly eight-day retreat, and a fair amount of *theological living* (faith-oriented reading plus lots of God/Church conversations) made me feel I *had* a real religious life. And I did. The question for me had become instead: was I fully *living* a Christian vocation? The answer to that is much more complex. For simplicity's sake, let me say that I have learned more clearly that a Christian vocation is not equivalent to simply belonging to a religious order. To use an analogy, a Christian marriage is different from being Catholic and married with children.

My Christian vocation requires that I daily open myself to Jesus and allow my actions, emotions, desires, loves, hurts, fears, and plans (especially my precious plans), to be shared with and shaped by Jesus' influence. Sharing means that I submit myself to Jesus and let Him have a say in what I am doing and who I am daily becoming, what I hold on to and what I relinquish. Acting in a Christian way means that I no longer belong to myself. Rather, I belong to Christ.

Some good friends of mine who have been married for several years recently shared with me one of the biggest adjustments they have had to make as a result of being married. They can no longer make plans in blissful isolation but have to consult with each other about practically every aspect of their lives. This consultative sharing can be both a joy and an annoyance. Each one is called out of the prison of their own ego and invited to love, sacrifice, and make adjustments so that the other can grow and flourish. We really grow when we are called out of ourselves. But there is joy in sharing intimately in the life of the Beloved. We are created for the joy of sharing intimately in the life of the other. We are made in the image and likeness of God who *is relationship*.

A Christian vocation requires an intimate relationship with Christ. It requires making this relationship a priority on a *daily* basis. *Sacred Story* prayer, more than any other spiritual discipline I have encountered in my forty years in religious life, brings me face-to-face with Christ in a relationship that calls me out of myself. It is the most effective path that has enabled me to be true to the man and priest that God desires me to be. It is not always easy and I do not want to minimize the challenge it has been in terms of my honesty and openness. It is a joy and an annoyance for exactly the same reasons as any serious relational commitment. I have had moments of aggravation and difficulty in praying *Sacred Story*. I have also experienced times when I did not want to pray because I knew I would be confronted with things I would prefer to ignore.

Here is a typical example. Some time ago, I was struggling internally with someone who, I judged, had wronged me. I was hurt, frustrated, and upset from what I perceived to be an injustice against myself. I discovered I was not at all upset when this person experienced misfortunes, for I felt this person *deserved* it. In prayer, I was not speaking with Jesus about this person. Instead I found myself rehearsing conversations in my head about how I had been wronged. My focus was on myself.

One day I was awakened to my lack of Christian charity. Instinctively I understood that I needed to bring my feelings about this person to Jesus and yet, I resisted. A part of my heart wanted to simply rehearse my justified hurts. It took several *Sacred Story* prayer periods for me to begin to speak *from my heart* to Christ about what I was feeling. The *insight* that I needed to reach out and forgive this person came in a split-second. I was also able to accept some of the fault lines in my own personality which may have contributed to the initial difficulties. It is amazing how that clarity comes with honesty. This was a *graced* experience!

However, upon leaving the time of *Sacred Story* prayer, a new inspiration took hold. Perhaps it is unwise to forgive? I could lose ground. The re-emerging frustration and darkened spirit—the counter-inspiration—accompanying this new inspiration was in *marked* contrast to the peacefulness I had experienced previously in the time of *Sacred Story* prayer. In testing the spiritual inspirations, it was clear which inspiration was from the Divine-Inspirer and which inspiration was from the counter-inspirer. Honestly, I was strongly tempted to *ignore* the truth of my spiritual discernment and go with the refusal to forgive. But I was being invited by God to *disarm*. I was invited to be vulnerable. It was an invitation to greater spiritual freedom, the freedom that Ignatius calls *detachment*. Freedom *sounds* good, but it is not something we always really want.

This event was a wake-up call because it clearly presented the difficult choice of forgiveness. It may sound odd but it gave me the conviction that Jesus is interested in *everything* I am doing. Every thought, word and deed I have is important to Christ. He wants to be part of everything I experience. *Sacred Story*, prayed faithfully, has made me aware of what *being in relationship* with Jesus means. I feel the effects of the surrender that is necessary for a real relationship with Jesus, and I feel it in a particularly powerful way twice a day. I have chosen to make spiritual surrender the center of my Jesuit life. And praying *Sacred Story* prayer has revealed how many areas of my daily life I keep off-limits from Christ.

A strong intellectual tradition is a characteristic of the Society of Jesus; it is a good in and of itself. But there is something that Ignatius wanted Jesuits to value above learning: virtue, the spiritual life, and the surrender of our will and our hearts to Christ. The human gifts we cultivate only reach their fruitfulness in light of a well-grounded spiritual life. In Section Ten of the Jesuit Constitutions, entitled "How the Whole

Body of the Society is to be Preserved and Increased in its Well-being," Ignatius says:

Thus it appears that care should be taken in general that all the members of the Society devote themselves to the solid and perfect virtues and to spiritual pursuits, and attach greater importance to them than to learning and other natural and human gifts. For these interior gifts are necessary to make those exterior means efficacious for the end which is being sought.

(Part X [813] 2.)

This advice is written for Jesuits, and for the care and growth of the Society of Jesus. Yet it offers good pragmatic Ignatian wisdom that is applicable to any vocation or situation in the Church. Human gifts and qualities reach their perfection and the height of their potency when the bearer of those gifts and/or qualities is grafted to the vine of Christ—when they surrender to Christ. This holds true for the talents of the athlete, the intellectual acumen of the college student, the artistic skills of the singer or architect, the healing gifts of the doctor or nurse, the ministry of religious and priests, the leadership skills of the politician and the professional business person, and the love of husband and wife for each other and their children.

The personal decision I face daily—twice daily—is how much of my life will I allow to be grafted onto the vine of Christ? How much will I allow myself to *abide* in His Love? Jesus must have been looking at grapevines when He spoke this passage from John's Gospel. The vine or stalk is the source of all nutrients. Only shoots which grow directly from it, or have been grafted onto it, bear fruit. As I look back over my life, I can see that I have produced all sorts of fruit by my *own* effort. What has become a much more important question at this point is: how much of what I produce is the fruit of my relationship with Jesus? In other words, have I allowed myself to become a "daily disciple" of Jesus by being in relationship with Him? Am I grafted onto the vine of Christ?

The bottom line of my experience of *Sacred Story* is that I am being challenged to open *all* of my heart and my life to God's grace. While the commitment to the Jesuits and the priesthood always felt full-time and lifelong, the *relationship* with Jesus seemed to have an on-again, off-again feel to it. Quite frankly, I was more in control than Christ. Now I feel that I have truly begun to commit to *Jesus*. Twice daily I need to come to Him with my ups and downs, my joys and angers, my loves and victories, my failures and grief, and my *constant* need.

My *constant* need: what does that mean? It means that *Sacred Story* prayer makes me more aware of my weakness, my failures, and my need for redemption. I have been graced with the eyes to see the reason for Christ's redeeming sacrifice, more clearly than ever before. It is a sacrifice and grace I cannot live without. Perhaps it is the same discovery of the alcoholic or drug addict. One day, the addict finally wakes up and realizes that the life they thought they controlled is actually out of control.

The only way to salvation is to surrender to love's sobriety and embrace. The alcoholic genuinely in touch with the truth of her/his life knows they are *always recovering* and are never *fully* recovered. One must live constantly with the knowledge of her/his vulnerability and turn to God for help and aid. It is a life of submission, humility, and holy dependence.

Is the invitation to submission, humility and holy dependence the best way for me to convince you to stay committed to *Sacred Story* prayer? Is this good marketing? Perhaps not, but I am convinced that while your issues may be different from mine, your experience will pull you into the same position of humility, submission, and dependency on God when confronted with the truth of your weakness and need.

What could possibly be attractive about living this way? Praying and living *Sacred Story* enables a person to be vulnerable, humbly submissive and dependent on God. I can rely on Jesus, who has promised to give me what I need: "If you remain in me and my words remain in you, ask for whatever you want and it will be done for you." (Jn 15: 7)

These words utterly change a person and their world view. Jesus offers this relationship so that my joy "may be full." How so? Because I experience that even in the weakest and most vulnerable condition of my life, Love does not walk away from me. Love has irrevocably committed Himself to me. He sacrificed for me so that I could be whole, and He wants the knowledge of this great love to be known by me on the most intimate level. He has also promised that this life of discipleship gives great glory to the Father in heaven. Allowing oneself to abide in His love will bear fruit that will give glory to the Father of Jesus Christ. What an awesome reality!

At the beginning of a retreat or in my daily *Sacred Story* prayer, I try to commit to this relationship. The renewal of my vocational commitment to Christ in the daily engagement with *Sacred Story* prayer is a means to deepen the knowledge of my radical dependence on God. It fosters the joy of a personal relationship with Christ Jesus that grounds me and opens me up to the deepest yearnings of my heart.

The more I open my heart to a serious relationship with Christ, the more I come to understand the joy for which I have been created You also have been created for this Joy. That is why I am confident you will remain in the embrace of *Sacred Story* and the Lord Jesus who loves you beyond all reckoning. The Love that grounds the universe holds you in His Heart.

ଓଃ

৪১

Glorious Lord Christ,…

You who are the first and the last,

The living and the dead and the risen again;

You who gather into your exuberant unity

Every beauty, every affinity, every energy,

Every mode of existence;

It is you to whom my being cried out with a desire

As vast as the universe,

'In truth you are my Lord and my God.'[10]

৪৩

A Note to Pastors and

Adult Faith Formation Directors

The Sacred Story Institute is working toward a full complement of parish resources for the *Whole-Life Confession* and the *Forty Weeks* programs. If you would like to help make this happen, please contact us at the email address on the following page. Also, please let us know what type of materials you would find helpful to make this resource more flexible for your use.

In the meantime, you will find very basic resources you need to use *Forty Weeks* for parish renewal, RCIA and prayer groups. Please access these resources at the member's site for 40 Week Parish Course at sacredstory.net. When you register as a member, you can access the program materials and the materials and the membership is free.

Seattle, USA
sacredstoryrpress.com

Sacred Story Press explores dynamic new dimensions of classic Ignatian spirituality, based on St. Ignatius' Conscience Examen in the *Sacred Story* prayer method pioneered by Fr. Bill Watson, S.J. We are creating a new class of spiritual resources. Our publications are research-based, authentic to the Catholic Tradition and designed to help individuals achieve integrated, spiritual growth and holiness of life.

We Request Your Feedback

The Sacred Story Institute welcomes feedback on *Forty Weeks*. Contact us via email or letter. Give us ideas, suggestions and inspirations for how to make this a better resource for Catholics and Christians of all ages and walks of life.

For bulk orders and group discounts, contact us:
admin-team@sacredstory.net

Sacred Story Institute & Sacred Story Press
1401 E. Jefferson Suite 405
Seattle, Washington, 98122

About the Author

Fr. William Watson, S.J., D. Min., has spent over thirty-five years developing Ignatian programs and retreats He has collaborated extensively with Fr. Robert Spitzer in the last fifteen years on Ignatian retreats for corporate CEO's. In the spring of 2011 he launched a non profit institute to bring Ignatian Spirituality to Catholics of all ages and walks of life. The Sacred Story Institute is promoting third millennium evangelization for the Society of Jesus and the Church by using the time-tested *Examination of Conscience* of St. Ignatius.

Fr. Watson has served as: Director of Retreat Programs at Georgetown University; Vice President for Mission at Gonzaga University; and Provincial Assistant for International Ministries for the Oregon Province of the Society of Jesus. He holds Masters Degrees in Divinity and Pastoral Studies, respectively (1986; Weston Jesuit School of Theology, Cambridge Massachusetts). He received his Doctor of Ministry degree in 2009 from The Catholic University of America (Washington D.C.).

Endnotes

1 Paul Doncoeur, SJ, *The Heart of Ignatius*, (Baltimore: Helicon, 1959), 34.

2 The image on this page is from My Sacred Story Missal, (Seattle: Sacred Story Press, 2015), 58.

3 Gabor Maté, *In the Realm of Hungry Ghosts: Close Encounters with Addiction* (Berkeley: North Atlantic Books, 2010), 136-7.

4 If you feel called, you can reflect on the entire Decalogue as enumerated in the *Catechism of the Catholic Church* (CCC, 561-672). You can either purchase an inexpensive paperback or you can access the text online:

http://www.vatican.va/archive/ccc_css/archive/catechism/p3s2c1a1.htm

5 If you feel called, you can reflect on the entire Decalogue as enumerated in the *Catechism of the Catholic Church* (CCC, 561-672). You can either purchase an inexpensive paperback or you can access the text online:

http://www.vatican.va/archive/ccc_css/archive/catechism/p3s2c1a1.htm

6 The image on this page is from My Sacred Story Missal, (Seattle: Sacred Story Press, 2015), 13.

7 *Catechism of the Catholic Church (CCC) 1469--John Paul II, RP 31, 5.*

8 The image on this page is from My Sacred Story Missal, (Seattle: Sacred Story Press, 2015), 43.

9 "Abide in Me" is taken from the afterword to Fr. Watson's work: *Forty Weeks: An Ignatian Path to Christ with Sacred Story Prayer*

10 Thomas M. King, SJ, *Teilhard's Mass: Approaches to The Mass on the World* (Mahwah: Paulist Press, 2005) 120.

Made in the USA
Columbia, SC
17 May 2019